A Hoxton Childhood
&
The Years After

A. S. Jasper

A HOXTON
CHILDHOOD
&
THE YEARS
AFTER

A. S. JASPER

Illustrated by
JAMES BOSWELL
&
JOE McLAREN

Spitalfields Life
Books

This edition first published in 2017 by Spitalfields Life Books Ltd

1

A Hoxton Childhood was first published in monthly instalments
in *Profile, Magazine of the Hackney Library Service* between
October 1967 and September 1968, and subsequently in one
volume by Barrie & Rockliff in 1969 when it was accompanied
by James Boswell's illustrations

In previous editions of *A Hoxton Childhood*, the protagonists
were given fictional names to protect the identities of their
counterparts in life but here we have used their real names
consistent with A. S. Jasper's practice in *The Years After*

This is the first publication of *The Years After*

The portraits of William, Johanna and Stanley Jasper were taken
in 1922

A CIP catalogue for this book is available from the British Library

ISBN 978-0-9957401-0-5

A Spitalfields Life Book
Edited by The Gentle Author

Designed by David Pearson
Typeset in Miller Text

Printed by Legatoria Editoriale Giovanni Olivotto Spa
Viale Dell'Industria 2
36100 Vicenza
Italy

Published by
Spitalfields Life Books Ltd
16 Victoria Cottages
Spitalfields
London E1 5AJ

www.spitalfieldslife.com
@thegentleauthor

CONTENTS

To My Mother
and to all mothers of that time

William Jasper

Johanna Jasper

Stanley Jasper

A HOXTON CHILDHOOD

Illustrated by
JAMES BOSWELL

CHAPTER ONE

'I always told you he's no bleeding good and nothing good will come of it if they get married.'

Those were my father's words after discovering my sister Mary was four months pregnant. This knowledge came to my parents' notice due to the following circumstances.

One Sunday evening my mother and father had gone for their Sunday night drink – my eldest sister Mary was with Gerry her boyfriend. My older brother Bert was out scrounging with his friends somewhere in Hoxton, and my second eldest sister Florrie was also out with friends. My baby sister Amelia was with Mother and Father outside the pub in a pram. This left me with Mary and Gerry alone in the house.

I suddenly heard Mary and Gerry having a terrific row, and Gerry slammed out of the house. Mary was crying her eyes out. She was still crying when she called me to the kitchen.

'Stan, would you go to the chemist for me?'

I asked her what I had to get, and she gave me a blue bottle and asked me to get 'twopennyworth of spirits of salts.' I was only about eight years old at the time and didn't know the difference between spirits of salts or medicine of any sort.

In those days, 1913, a chemist was open in Hoxton until late on Sunday nights. Off I went. At that time we were living in Canal Road, and I only had to walk into Hyde Road then I was in the Hoxton market.

To get to the chemist I had to pass the Kings Arms public house; this was situated in the narrow way of Hoxton.

As I passed, I saw my mother standing in the passageway of the pub.

1

'Whatever are you doing out this time of the night?' said my mother.

I had to tell her where I was going and what I had to get. When she heard my story she was livid.

'Give me that bloody bottle,' and there was a crash as she slung it in the road.

My father was having a drink in the bar with his pal.

'Bill,' Mum called out. 'I want you a minute.'

Out came Dad. My mother explained why I was there, and they decided to go home and see what it was all about.

On arriving home they found Mary lying on her bed, still crying. My mother eventually got the story from her. It seemed Gerry had a rough home life and some months previous Mum had let him have a room, but it looked as if he spent more time in my sister's room than he did in his own. My father always reckoned Gerry was a small-time crook, his reason being Gerry would depart from the house about 4 am and come home at all times during the day. When the old man asked him why he kept such erratic hours, Gerry's answer was that he worked in the fish market.

Anyhow, to get back to the beginning. It was decided that whatever Gerry's failings he would have to marry my sister Mary. Gerry never came back that night so it was decided to wait until next day to work things out.

Before going on with the story I think I should give you a description of my family.

My father was about forty years of age at the time; he had a distinct Roman nose, a full moustache, slightly bandy legs and drooping shoulders. His main object in life was to be continually drunk, and he had every opportunity to keep that way. His job was delivering overmantels and small furniture to various places in East London. He used to go out at five in the morning. First call was the local pub for rum and milk; this he could keep up all day. He always had money; of every three articles he delivered, one was nicked, and the proceeds shared among the men who loaded him up. But at home he was tight with his money. I don't ever remember my mother having a week's wages off him – six or seven shillings was the most she ever received.

The reason he never gave her regular wages was he knew my mother could always earn a few shillings with her machine. To me, my mother was the most wonderful woman on earth. I find it hard to describe the love that she gave us. She had come to this country at the age of eighteen. Her family were musicians and had played at the royal Dutch Court. I never discovered why they emigrated – probably thought they could do better here.

When I was old enough to understand, I asked her what made her marry a man like my father. She told me that he had taken her out many times, but she always had to be home early for my grandmother was very strict. Eventually one night he brought her home past midnight and Grandmother refused to open the door. Consequently, he took her to his own place, made her pregnant and they had to get married. He deceived her from the start; she never got over the fact that he gave her a brass wedding ring.

At the time this story starts she had had six children and she loved every one of us. My eldest brother Will I never knew much about – he joined the Navy at fifteen and a half.

My eldest sister Mary, like all working girls at that time, went to work in a factory and went out at nights. She was small in build, not awfully good looking, and dressed better than most girls because Mum always made her dresses and skirts.

My brother Bert was a roamer and a local tough. I don't remember much of him at the time. He was about fifteen, and he was always out. Mum was so afraid of the company he kept that she had him put on a training ship at fifteen and a half. It definitely kept him from going crooked.

My second sister Florrie was very different. Since my earliest memories I was always with her. She would take me to school, and would come for me at four and I was allowed to sit next to her in class until four-thirty. She was very good looking and had fair wavy hair. She was always at my mother's call and for years was her right hand in helping in the house and helping sell the articles of clothing Mum made.

I was about eight years old at the time and rather a big boy for my age. My sisters used to make a fuss of me and my mother would hardly let me out of her sight. I dearly loved my mother, and now at sixty years of age her memory and love are still with me.

This leaves us with the baby of the family, Amelia, three years old, very pretty with golden curls. I well remember the day she was born.

We were living then at number three Clinger Street, Hoxton, in a hovel on the ground floor. It comprised two rooms and a kitchen, with an outside lavatory which also served the family upstairs. I was five years old. My mother and father and myself slept in the front room. My sister Mary was fifteen and my sister Florrie was eleven. They slept in the back room in one iron bedstead, with brother Bert who was thirteen in the same room. Being only a small child, I used to sleep against the wall, next to my mother in my parents' bed.

In the summer we lived in the kitchen, which had a stone floor, an old iron cooking range and was very dark. In the winter it was very cold and damp so we lived in the front room where my mother and father slept. For lighting we had gas brackets with 'fish tail' burners. It was a terrible crush when we were all home having our meals in the bedroom.

August 17th, 1910, was a very hot day. About eleven o'clock that morning my sister Florrie was told to take me out and play in the playground, which was situated somewhere at the back of Hammond Square School. I remember seeing a lot of activity going on in the house that morning. The lady upstairs was doing a lot of running around and I also remember seeing a nurse arrive with a black Gladstone bag. My sister kept me out until she thought it was time for dinner – not that we ever had much. When we arrived home, she told me to wait outside and she would come and tell me when it was all right for me to come in.

A few moments later she came out for me.

'Come and have a look at what Mum has bought you.'

As I entered the door I could hear a baby crying. My little sister Amelia had been born while I was out playing. My eyes must have opened wide in wonderment as I was lifted up to see the new baby. My mother told my sister Florrie to lay me next to her, as I started to cry. My mother cuddled me up close to her in her efforts to stop me crying. She had always made such a fuss of me, and I suppose I must have realised my nose had been put out of joint. I never left my mother all that day. My sister got the room tidied up and my grandmother came. My sister was sent to the Kings Arms, a public house my father used in Hoxton, about eight o'clock that night to tell him to come home as Mum had been 'confined'. He eventually came home more drunk than sober. I hardly ever remember him being sober. He didn't seem to show much interest in the baby and after a while went out again.

Came time for going to bed. My mother told me I would have to sleep with my sister Florrie as I was now getting a 'big boy'. Also, I could not sleep with her in the big bed because of the baby. I cried and cried my eyes out. It was understood. I had never known anything else. I had always slept in my parents' bed. In the end, I must have been pacified and went with my sister Florrie. She laid me in her bed and quickly got in beside me and tried to cuddle me off to sleep. I must have gone to bed sobbing my heart out at leaving my mother. In the room was a small paraffin lamp. They were bought for a penny. I remember waking up in the night and seeing the shadows that were cast by the lamp as the flame moved. I cried out in fright. Everyone woke up, including my parents. My father was swearing and shouting, 'Keep that bloody kid quiet, can't yer.'

In the end, my mother shouted through the thin walls to 'Bring him in here.' My sister carried me in and my father was still in a rage, swearing and shouting in his half-drunken stupor. My mother placed a pillow at the foot of the bed, and laid me down to sleep. Feeling her next to me, I soon went off.

Next morning I was dressed and taken out again to play because the nurse was coming. After she had been I went in to my mother and refused to leave her. I also wanted to be with my new sister. Twelve o'clock came and my father came in.

'What brings you home at this time of day?' my mother asked.

He had never been known to come home at midday, hence my mother's question. He explained that his mates at work had collected a few shillings for a colleague whose baby had just died, and was being buried that afternoon. He had to take it to Wilmer Gardens where the chap lived.

My mother asked him to take me with him as the lady upstairs was coming down to clean up. Reluctantly, he took me with him. I had not the slightest idea what it was all about. He held me by the hand and took me to a block of broken-down tenement dwellings at the top left-hand side of Wilmer Gardens.

They were directly opposite North's Lodging House. These tenements were set back well away from the road and they were rat-infested. To get to the front entrance, one had to cross a vast square of waste ground. In the summer, this was just a dust and rubbish heap. In the winter, it was a sea of mud and filth. The front doors of the tenements, or what was left of them, were always open. Dirty and half-starved children were playing in the filth and garbage that had collected outside. To get to the flat of my father's workmate we had to climb a flight of rickety stairs. As we passed the other flats on our way up, I could smell the nauseating odours that came from the rooms. I could hear some of the occupants swearing and rowing and children crying.

We eventually reached our destination, and were told to come in the open door. I still remember my father's friend telling him how his little son had died. It could have only been a few weeks old. His eyes were red with crying. The remaining children were sitting around a wooden table with newspaper for a tablecloth.

After my father gave him the few shillings he had collected, he was asked if he would like to see the baby before the undertaker arrived to screw down the coffin. I believe it was the thing everyone did in those days. My father said he would and told me to stay put.

6

This I would not do. I held on to his hand and insisted on going with him. After giving me a scolding, he told me I could come with him.

On an old chest-of-drawers in a room with three beds in was a little white coffin. My father's friend slid back the lid and amid tears said to my father, 'What about him, Bill?' meaning me.

My father replied, 'He's all right,' and beckoning to me, said, 'Come and have a look, boy.' He lifted me up to see the dead baby.

I have never forgotten that face. In my tiny childish mind, I got my first glimpse of peace.

But to get back to the story of Mary and Gerry. On the Monday Gerry was sent for, my father's instructions were: 'If he don't come I'll bleeding well come and get him.' I think my brother Bert went with the message on the Monday night. Gerry arrived. He was a short corpulent chap, thin fair hair, heavy jowls on his face, thought the world of himself, and was prepared for a fight with my father. Although my sister had been courting him for some time, he had never been in our company much. On the two or three times he had been with us he never left a very good impression.

After a terrific argument and several threats by Gerry and my father to punch each other's heads in, it was decided that the wedding would take place.

First, where were they going to live? They couldn't live with us – we already had a couple with three children upstairs. It was agreed that Mother would try to find a bigger house.

In those days it was easy; one only had to go to an agent, pay the first week's rent and move in. On more than one occasion my father came home late, drunk as usual, and was told by the next-door neighbours we didn't live there any more. We had owed so much rent that the agent had threatened to throw us in the road if we didn't pay up.

On this occasion it wasn't that we owed so much rent but the fact we had to have a larger house. My mother duly found and inspected a house in Salisbury Street, New North Road. It wasn't a bad area and I always remember it was the nicest house we ever had.

Mary said she would like the top front room. Gerry agreed it would be fine and it was duly decided to take it. My father wasn't consulted on moving. It hardly mattered to him where he lived, he was hardly ever in; so long as a pub was near he didn't care.

The moving was to take place on the following Saturday afternoon. My brother Bert was detailed to 'go and get a barrow' on the Saturday morning. This was got from a local costermongers. A deposit of two shillings was required and the barrow was ours for the day. If we returned it before nine at night we were given one and sixpence back.

After dinner on the Saturday the move started. Gerry hadn't arrived after promising to be there early. My mother supervised the packing and tying up of the bedding. It must have been a good twenty minutes' walk from Canal Road to Salisbury Street, so one can guess the amount of journeys that had to be done. Loads were packed and tied on that barrow that only Eastern labourers would attempt to move. Midway through moving, Gerry arrived.

'What time do you call this?' my mother asked him.

His reply was, 'I had to work late in the fish market.' Gerry just could not tell the truth. It was discovered afterwards that a neighbour had seen him playing pitch-and-toss in a gambling school in Wilmer Gardens, a notorious place for local villains and petty criminals. It boasted of a lodging house which housed them; often after a crime in Hoxton, the police would turn the inmates out to see if the suspects were there.

Gerry did his share of pulling the barrow and we eventually finished about 9.30pm. Mary and Florrie got cracking on putting up the beds and undoing bundles. Gerry helped, but tried every now and then to snatch a quick snog with Mary. In the end he gave up; too many of us were running all over the house putting things in various rooms.

About eleven it was decided we had had enough. My mother made cocoa and cut bread and butter which we set into with gusto; having had nothing to eat since dinnertime, we were all ravenously hungry. Gerry was asked to stay but declined. Since the discovery of my sister's pregnancy he was not on very good terms with my father. Whenever they met, they eyed each other like two punch-drunk boxers waiting for the first blow to fall. My mother's patience somehow seemed to delay any fighting tactics. Anyhow, Gerry promised to come Sunday to tea.

Sunday morning we all got up early and put the house in ship-shape order. Before dinner I was instructed to go to Pimlico Walk which is the top end of Hoxton. This was an alleyway, next to the old Britannia Theatre. One could buy almost anything in the Walk on Sunday. I had to get a pint of winkles and a pennyworth of watercress. These constituted the main items for Sunday tea. Usually the old man would come in drunk, have his dinner and then go and sleep it off until tea-time. Woe-betide the peace of the household if there were no winkles and watercress. I've seen him create something awful. He would come downstairs, sit down at the table and say, 'No cress and winkles; you know bloody well I always have them.' Then the trouble would start: we kids were always terrified and immediately went to our mother's side. She would stand so much from him that in the end her patience was exhausted. Mum was quiet and would try by all means to talk him down. When this failed, she would go berserk and clump the old man for all she was worth. I've seen her rip the shirt off his back; he'd finish up with just the collar-band round his neck.

But to get back to the occasion of the first Sunday tea in the new house. Everything went very smoothly during tea. Gerry ate as though he had eaten nothing for weeks. The old man asked Gerry what his job in the fish market was.

'Portering,' said Gerry.

'Why don't you bring home a bit of fish now and then?' said the old man.

'I can always do that, Bill,' said Gerry, who was now trying to be good friends by calling my father by his Christian name. 'I'll drop some in as I knock off tomorrow.'

After tea the old man got ready for his visit to the local pub; at seven he was off. Gerry entertained the family with a few card tricks; he certainly could manipulate the cards. About nine o'clock my mother suggested plans should be worked out for the forthcoming wedding as time was getting near. It was agreed that the next day, after work, Mary and Gerry would go and put the banns up. My sisters were beginning to get a little excited at the prospect of the wedding. After all, Mary was the first one in the family to get wed and Mum was sure to see only the best was good enough. So there the discussion ended and we were all looking forward to the excitement and preparation in the forthcoming weeks.

Monday afternoon Gerry came round on a bike.

'Here you are, Ma,' he said, and gave Mum four big herrings wrapped in newspaper.

'Thanks, Gerry,' said Mum.

'They're straight from the market, Ma, so they're nice and fresh.'

Mum made him a cup of tea and asked him where he got his bicycle from. Since he had been calling in of late we noticed on two or three occasions he had a different bike.

'I managed to pick it up cheap, Ma, and hope to do it up, sell it and make a few bob,' Gerry replied.

If Mum was suspicious she kept it to herself. I remember this all so well because I was not at school; we had not had time to get me initiated at a local school since moving.

Towards seven o'clock that night my father came home and wanted to know what arrangements had been made for the wedding.

'I still don't think he's any cop and cannot see any good coming of this,' said the old man.

He'd had a few beers or rums and was in his usual aggressive mood.

'Don't talk that way,' said Mum, 'he's not a bad chap and he does work in the fish market. Just look what he brought home today.'

Mum got the four herrings from the larder to show him.

The old man picked up a herring, looked at it in disgust, and with, 'He don't bleeding well fool me, mate,' slung it back on the plate. 'He don't work in no bloody fish market. Probably bought them on a stall in Hoxton to make it look good.'

Mum started to cook the herrings and I noticed the old man didn't refuse his one. But he never altered his mind about Gerry. He treated him with suspicion, and always would.

The three weeks ahead were looked forward to with excitement and anticipation. First, the house had to be decorated; my mother and sister set into this with gusto. Wallpaper was about threepence a roll; a ball of whitening and boiled size made the whitewash for the ceiling. Gerry did his own room up. This he called the 'Bridal Suite'. When they had finished it looked very nice. Of all the houses we ever lived in (and we lived in plenty) this was the nicest and most homely place in my memory. Upstairs in the front was a large bedroom, Mary and Gerry's. At the back, another bedroom which my mother and father used. On the right-hand side was a fantastically large room which went from front to back of the house. It was over a stable. This the children used. A curtain divided the room in two halves, one half for my sisters and the other for my brother and myself. Four iron bedsteads and an old dressing-table were the furnishings. Downstairs was a front room (parlour if one had anything to put in it), at the rear a living room with kitchen range and a wash house adjoining. A small garden added to our pleasure. All this and rates paid for eight shillings a week.

After decorating, Gerry said he would like to keep fowls. My mother offered no resistance to this, but the old man, as usual, got his back up at the thought. Gerry got over this by offering to take him out for a drink at the Bridport Arms – this was the local pub, only at the end of the street and very convenient for the old man. On their return, permission was duly granted and next day Gerry built his chicken house. I must say he made it very attractive; he whitewashed the inside and painted the outside green. It was so nice that I as a child envied the chickens.

On the Sunday, I went with Gerry down Petticoat Lane to see what was going cheap in the chicken line. After inspecting every stall, we finished up with one hen which, after a lot of bargaining, Gerry got for four shillings. Under Gerry's arm went the hen and we safely got it home. The first day home it laid an egg. I shall never forget the look on Gerry's face. For months after, it was his pride and joy.

A conference was called which consisted of Mum, my sisters and Gerry's mother and father, in order to make arrangements for the coming wedding which was not far off now. It was the first time we had met Gerry's parents. His mother was a large woman with a thin face and her hair tied up in a knot at the back. She had had a very hard life. Her first husband had died when her four children were very young. When the oldest was about fourteen years she married again. Her husband was Gerry's stepfather. It seemed he was cruel to the children and ill-treated his wife. Consequently, when they were old enough to go to work they left home one after the other.

Gerry's stepfather was a huge man. A fish fryer by trade, he carried the scars of his job all over his arms. They were one mass of scars due to burning oil splashes. His face was horrible. My sister Florrie called him Battered Face (she usually had a nickname for everyone). His face seemed all bashed in. This, Gerry told us, was caused by fighting and brawling in his younger days. His right eye looked natural, but the left was glazed, and looked like an eye without a pupil. I never got near him. He used to terrify me.

Anyhow, it was agreed that they would come to the wedding and would help where they could with food, crockery, glasses and all things that were needed. What about music? They had a gramophone and records. The latest model with disc records. This was out of the blue. We only had a phonograph with 'cylinder' records. We gratefully accepted the loan of the gramophone.

'Could anyone play a mouth organ?' 'Yes,' we said. My eldest brother was coming home on leave from the Navy for the wedding, and he was an expert. Now we were all set for the great day regarding music.

After the conference ended, Battered Face invited all to a drink at the Bridport. All parted good friends and they arranged to see us all on Sunday fortnight at 9.30 am.

The next two weeks were a hard time for my mother. She was trying to give a good show for my sister but lacked the necessary cash to do all she would have liked. One day, she called my father in the front room and said, 'Bill, I'd like an overmantel in here, how much can you get one for?' He could have got one for nothing. As I have already explained, his job was delivering these things and being in a swindle at work, with his two mates, there was no question of paying. He said he could not get one 'under twenty-five shillings' and he must have the cash first, otherwise 'no deal'. Mum paid him and, as time went on, got rather worried when no over-mantel showed up. Two days before the wedding she threatened to 'brain him' if it did not show up in time. He delivered it next day. He knew her threat would be carried out.

The wedding date was also near my birthday. I had been prom-ised a watch if I would continue to be a 'good boy'. In Bridport Place there was a pawnshop by the name of Long & Doughty. If one took goods there to pawn, the local saying was, 'A long time in and doubt if they ever come out'. In those days nearly everyone had to go to pawn. One day, Mum wanted a few bob and took a parcel of clothes and bedsheets. It was fascinating to see the procedure. One went into a cubicle where the gent behind the counter usually knew his customers.

'How much?' were his first words.

'Ten shillings,' said Mum.

'Seven,' said the gent behind the counter.

'Oh Christ,' said Mum, 'don't be like that, Sid.'

'All right,' said Sid, 'I'll make it eight bob, but don't forget it's the last time I take this lot in.'

Mum had to settle for eight bob and Sid would then proceed as follows. He would pin the parcel up for storage with a very thick pin, then write out the ticket. Three tickets were needed. One to pin on the parcel, one for the record and one for the customer. The mechanism of the pen had to be seen to be believed. There were three inkwells for the three wire nibs, all controlled by the penholder. Sid would then proceed to write the tickets by picking up the penholder, dipping the three nibs in the three inkwells and then writing as though one ticket. One halfpenny was deducted from the loan for the ticket. On Saturday, if the parcel was required, I would be sent to Long & Doughty to redeem it. First, one handed in the ticket. This was placed in a small bag and hauled up by a piece of rope by whoever was working upstairs. When the parcel was found, it would come down the hatch with a crash. Sid would call out the name on the ticket and I would shout out 'One' or 'Two' according to the number of parcels there were. On redemption, the interest charge was one halfpenny per two shillings per month.

To get back to my watch I was going to have for my birthday. Coming out of the pawnshop, I saw a silver pocket watch marked up for four and ninepence. I told Mum I would like one just like that. She was a good sort and suggested we go in and have a look. This we did and not having the cash to spare, Sid behind the counter suggested we 'pay off' and get it when we paid the balance. Mum paid a shilling deposit and promised me I would have it in time for the wedding. Mum kept her promise. I got the watch a day before Mary's wedding. What happened to it I will tell later.

It was decided that my brother Bert and I were to have new suits. Bert was never worried about clothes. One of his objects in life was swimming. This he would do in the local canal every night in the summer. Crowds used to gather to watch the boys perform, and Bert would dive off the bridge for a ha'penny or off 'the Pipe' – a waste-water duct that was higher – for a penny. He was always coming home with some of his clothes missing. It was either a shirt or his boots. While the lads were swimming, the rogues would go round the heaps of clothes and help themselves. I always remember one night in particular. It got very late and Bert hadn't arrived home. Near midnight he crept in without his trousers. He had to wait until it was dark and the streets deserted before he could venture home. Consequently, Mum was never worried too much regarding his clothes.

Anyhow, a local tallyman was contacted and Bert and I had a new suit. I am sure it was the first new suit he ever had in his life. My sisters were more fortunate. Mum could always make them dresses. They also worked very hard getting the place in order, and Gerry continued to call in at all times. But he always had a different bike, 'one he had bought cheap and was going to do up', he would say.

We now come to the day before the wedding. We were all getting excited, and a feeling of jollity was in the air. My eldest brother came home on leave from the Navy and was going to be best man. He was a tall, good-looking chap, and well he knew it. He immediately took a firm dislike to Gerry. Why, I don't know.

Gerry was a rough diamond, but apart from the mystery surrounding the way he got his living, I could never see any reason to dislike him. The house was all in order and prepared for the next day's celebration. Being Saturday night, all retired to the Bridport Arms for a pre-celebration drink. Towards closing time the trouble started. My father, brother, Gerry and several friends were drinking up; Gerry was well away. He was also well aware of my brother's feelings towards him. The old man's feeling of animosity towards Gerry was sunk with the rum and beer he was drinking.

'Come on, Gerry, drink up,' my father said.

'Watch it, Dad, he's only a boy,' replied my brother.

That did it. Gerry immediately got his back up. 'Who are you calling a boy? I'm old enough to give you a bleeding good hiding,' and right away a fight started. Fists and pints were flying all over the place. Gerry really got stuck in. Someone ran home to my mother and sisters to tell them what was happening. They all went in the pub, managed to get order restored and finally coaxed them to come home. Mum told them they should be ashamed of themselves. For bridegroom and best man to fight the night before the wedding was terrible. Mum had two arms that were like large legs of mutton and when they saw her begin to roll her sleeves up they knew it was time to call a halt. Friendship was restored by opening up one of the several gallon jars of ale that had been got in for the wedding. All wished each other the best of luck and all ended well. Brother Will shook hands with Gerry before he left and promised he wouldn't be late in the morning. They parted the best of pals.

There wasn't much sleep that night. Very early in the morning my sisters got up and made tea and started preparing for the great day. The wedding was at 10 am. This did not leave a lot of time for formalities. It was a walking wedding. Ten minutes to the church. After tea and toast, the old man came downstairs, still half dazed by the beer and the fight the night before. He didn't want anything to eat and so got stuck into a rum and milk and wanted to know 'how much bleeding longer' he would have to wait for the lavatory to be available. Mum dressed my young sister and myself and gave us strict instructions to keep ourselves clean and for me to look after Amelia. The old man started to get himself ready; he'd bought himself a pair of striped trousers and a bobtail coat, all second-hand from a stall in Hoxton market. My sisters just could not keep a straight face. I thought they were going in hysterics when he started to put on a collar and tie; he had never worn one in his life. They eventually got it on for him after a lot of swearing and blinding. The coat was going green from age. He did look a sight, with brown boots, striped trousers, a semi-green bobtail coat and a flat cap. But he was quite pleased with himself. What was good enough for the gentry was good enough for him, he insisted. My brother Bert looked a different boy; I had never seen him look so smart. My sisters looked good too. Florrie was dressed in a nice white blouse with a sailor collar and a white jabot in the front. Her hair was nice and wavy and she looked good. Mary was similarly dressed. It was the fashion in those days to wear 'skirt and blouse' for most occasions. She looked very nice. Mum looked nice too. I'll always remember her blue blouse trimmed with lace and a large cameo brooch.

My brother Will went off to meet Gerry while we all set off walking to the church. Being early on a Sunday morning there was hardly anyone about. We must have looked a sight as we walked along the street, especially the old man. My sisters were taking the mickey out of him all the way, but were careful not to let him notice.

We arrived in church and took our places. Gerry's mother and father arrived with several invited friends. My brother and Gerry were late arrivals. I can see Gerry to this day walking to the altar. I think everyone gasped for breath as he walked up the aisle. He had Bulldog-toe shoes, peg-top trousers, a silk sash round his stomach, white shirt, no collar, a large silk scarf tied in a double knot around his neck, with the ends tucked in his braces, a long coat with turn-back cuffs and pearl buttons and a flat cap like a pancake. All local 'boys' dressed like that in those days.

The marriage ceremony was duly performed. While Gerry and Mary were in the vestry, we all waited outside the church ready to pelt them with confetti. We then started to walk home. We were quite a crowd by now and if we looked a sight going, goodness knows what we looked like coming back. Mary was in front holding Gerry's arm. Gerry had his hands in his pockets, his long coat flapping from side to side with each step he took. The old man had had a few rums before leaving home and was well away in his bobtail with a large red handkerchief hanging out of the tail pocket. It didn't take us long to get home. I think my mother and my sister Florrie were a little embarrassed by the antics of the two nifty dressers and hurried them as quickly out of sight as they could. Mum and my sisters had set the wedding breakfast before going to church and it didn't take us long to get stuck in. Everyone was drinking and good luck was wished by all to the bride and groom. After breakfast, all were set for a good time. Mum and my sisters cleared away and started to prepare dinner. A leg of pork went in the oven with two chickens. Never in our natural lives had we known such times.

I was very happy; my watch was keeping good time and I suppose I was looking at it every five minutes. While dinner was being prepared my father suggested all the men retire to the front room for a 'wet', it being too early to go to the Bridport Arms. Their conversation was of a sporting nature. Boxers of the day were discussed. Bombardier Billy Wells, Jack Johnson, Tancy Lee and lots more. Prospects of the forthcoming Derby were also considered. Gerry reckoned he had a cert which was an outsider, much to the old man's disgust, who said 'the favourite just could not lose'.

On the Saturday before the wedding several gallons of ale and bottles of spirits had been ordered and delivered, and the old man suggested that this was the time to have a 'whip round' to pay for it. Everyone paid their share, and it was agreed that all would go to the Bridport to pay the bill as soon as they opened at twelve-thirty. It would also be a good opportunity to have a few before dinner. At twelve-thirty prompt, all male members were away. At one-thirty Gerry came back to the house and suggested all the females 'come up for a drink'. Gerry was getting well-oiled and in a very happy mood.

My young sister and I were standing at the front door as they all went out, when Gerry asked us if we would like an ice cream. He gave me fourpence to get two ices. Gerry had never given me fourpence all the time we had known him and I was beginning to hope the wedding would last for ever.

While everyone was up at the Bridport, my brother Bert was alone in the house with all the gallon jars of ale. He must have thought what was good enough for the grown-ups was good enough for him. He decided to try a half-pint. Eventually he decided to try another, and by the time Mum and all the females returned he was blind drunk. He was in a terrible state. Gerry's ma picked him up and laid him out in the garden and gave him soda-water to try and make him sick. It was decided to leave him there and let him sleep it off.

Dinner was ready to serve out, but the males were not home yet. I was detailed to go up the pub and ask them to come home. I managed to get my brother's eye and told them dinner was ready.

Would they come home immediately? If not, Mum was coming up herself to have them out. As soon as I mentioned 'Mum was coming', for the sake of peace they decided to come home. How they all managed to sit round the table, I'll never know. Nothing was impossible to my mother.

During dinner several people asked where Bert was. After Mum had explained what had happened, they all agreed it was best to leave him to try and sleep it off.

Everyone praised Mum for the dinner and all said it was the best they had ever had. My sisters started to clear away and several of the men wanted to go to the lavatory pretty urgently. The first one out was Gerry's stepfather. On trying to open the door, he found it was locked from the inside. He bashed on the door and roared, 'How long?'

It seemed during dinner my brother Bert had recovered enough to go to the lavatory and feeling sick and bad had locked himself in and was out to the wide.

My father and several others came out to see what all the shouting was about. Gerry started to bang on the door and shouted, 'Hurry up, Bert, my father wants to go.'

'Sod off,' said Bert, 'I feel sick.'

By now Gerry's stepfather was raving and threatened to 'bash the bleeding door in'.

'Go to your house and use your own closet,' said Bert.

'Ain't it all right,' said Gerry's stepfather. 'I'm expected to go all the bleedin' way to London Fields to use the soddin' lavvo.'

'We've got to get him out somehow,' said Gerry.

Eventually Mum arrived on the scene and somehow coaxed him 'to be reasonable'. She managed to get him to slide the bolt and when he emerged it was a sight for sore eyes.

He'd had diarrhoea very badly and was sick all over his new suit.

'That's the last bloody suit you'll ever get from me,' declared Mum. She was terribly annoyed. Mary and Florrie managed to get him inside and cleaned him up.

After that rumpus over the lavatory, things settled down to normal. Everyone was tired and it was decided that all the older guests should try to get some sleep in preparation for the party that night. I can't remember what became of Gerry and Mary – probably locked themselves in their 'Bridal Suite' as he called it.

I remember my father going to his own bed. As he took his trousers off, his money fell out of his pocket. He was so drunk he couldn't bend down to find it. I was going upstairs as this happened and looked in the door and saw some cash on the floor. Knowing he always kept Mum short, I dived under the bed and picked up a two-shilling piece. He didn't know it was me, but in his stupor he knew someone was there and threatened to 'bash their bleeding brains out' if he caught them. I slid out, found Mum and gave her the two shillings I managed to pick up. She asked me how I came by it, and I explained what had happened.

'Good boy,' she said, and upstairs she went. Dad was now out to the world, so she had all the silver and left him the coppers. When he woke up he never made any reference to his loss. Gerry's mother and father and several others went into our big bedroom to try and sleep. There was a lot of laughing and joking going on. Gerry's ma was telling his father not to 'try and take bleeding liberties' with her and to 'wait till he got to his own place'. After a while everyone seemed to doze off and all was quiet.

About five-thirty, Mum decided it was time to get tea ready. Nobody seemed to want much. The old man had his winkles and cress and was fighting fit. After tea everyone retired to the front room and the drinks were soon flowing. Florrie put the records on. We had the top hits of the day. 'See them Shuffling Along', 'Alexander's Ragtime Band', we had the lot.

My eldest brother's mate arrived and he immediately took up with my sister Florrie. They got the dancing going and everything was soon underway. Mum liked a waltz, and one of the male guests named George also liked to waltz. He was a nice-looking chap and he could dance. He took to Mum and they had several dances together.

After a while someone suggested a song. First to go was Gerry's stepfather. His song was 'I've fought and bled for England but what has she done for me?' This was all about a soldier returned from the wars crippled and unable to work and was reduced to begging in the streets. Battered Face sang in a voice that nearly busted all the looking-glasses in the new overmantel. All agreed it was 'bleedin' well sung' and he was invited to 'drink up'.

Meantime, I was still admiring my watch and thought how lucky I was to own such a masterpiece. My father had somehow managed to borrow an accordion. He always boasted he could play. All he could do was vamp on two notes. Anyhow, he did his stuff with a song called 'They're all very fine and large, some are fat and prime'. This was a ditty about a chap who goes to a common lodging house for a night's kip and comes out next morning running alive'o. The old man did all the actions like scratching himself and it went down well. Everyone said, 'Well done, Bill. What about another one?' He was only too happy to oblige with 'Across the Bridge at Midnight', accompanied by my brother on the mouth organ. This was a song about a gambler who had lost all his money at cards and thought about throwing himself in the river. The old man would have gone on for ever but he got shouted down as the younger ones wanted the gramophone.

Dancing started again and George suggested another waltz to Mum who was pleased to accept. By this time the old man was well out and was beginning to take a dim view of Mum dancing with George all night. When they had finished their dance, he sat down next to Mum and started nagging. She stuck it for as long as she possibly could and then suddenly picked up the shovel in the hearth and clouted him round the face. She called him all the 'miserable old gits' she could lay her tongue to. This started a real bust-up.

Everyone was on Mum's side and all agreed there was 'no harm in it'; George was prepared to settle it out in the road with the old man, which he readily agreed to. But he was dead crafty. To get out to the street he had to pass the stairs. As he reached them he shot up halfway, grabbed the banisters with one hand and offered to challenge anyone who came near him. He was in a commanding position to lash out with one fist and one boot. Mary was crying her eyes out. To think that the 'ole sod' should start a fight on her wedding day. Gerry's stepfather, who could have broken our old man in half, somehow got order and led him back to the front room. He gave him a drink and made him promise to behave himself. Soon everything seemed forgotten and everyone was drinking up again and dancing, but Mum and the old man were sitting glaring at each other and we were all afraid another fight was going to start.

I sat on Mum's knee and showed her my treasured watch. Mary and Florrie cut loads of sandwiches which were offered round with mustard pickles, pickled onions and gherkins. This seemed to quieten everyone down.

After the sandwiches Mary and Florrie sang their duet, 'When we went to school together' with mouth organ accompaniment, which was well received. The old man wanted to play the accordion again, but was promptly told to 'put the bloody thing down'. He had no alternative but to do just that.

'Come on, Gerry,' said his ma, 'give us G. H. Chirgwin.'

With a bulging neck and his eyes closed, Gerry gave a rendering of 'My Fiddle is My Sweetheart'. He then came forward with 'I am but a poor blind boy'. Tears flowed from Gerry's ma, but all agreed (including Gerry) that 'songs like that wanted a bit of singing'. My older brother finished up by singing a real heartbreaker called 'When I Lost You'.

The party was now getting tired and it was also late. Everyone had to see about getting a move on because of work tomorrow. All except Gerry. 'No bleeding work' was going to see him tomorrow. Gerry's ma and stepfather thanked Mum for such a wonderful time and hoped Gerry and Mary would make a go of things. They had to get the last bus to Homerton. Battered Face carried the gramophone and Gerry's ma the horn. Goodness knows how they managed to squeeze on a bus! We all went to bed tired. It had been a hectic day.

Early Monday morning my father staggered out at five o'clock. He started the day with his rum and milk, and then to work. Florrie gave us all a cup of tea about seven o'clock, taking care not to wake the bride and groom. Poor Mum was left to clear up the mess left over, with the despondent prospect of trying to make ends meet in the forthcoming week. This turned out to be a disaster for all. My watch went back to hock and Sid behind the counter generously lent Mum three shillings on it. I never saw it again. Next day, Gerry got pinched for stealing a bike. It just goes to show.

CHAPTER TWO

Things looked very bad for Gerry when he appeared in Court on a charge of stealing a bicycle. He had no previous convictions, but there had been such a spate of stolen bicycles that the magistrate was making an example of anyone who was caught. He was remanded and due to appear at Old Street Police Court the following Monday. My father kept on to Mum about Gerry being a thief. He forecast a criminal future for him. Yet who was a bigger rogue than he, himself? Mum reminded him of this and said the day would come when he would be caught, which he was.

Poor Mary was distraught. No money was coming in, and it was all left to my mother to help her, keep us all, pay the rent and do everything in general. To get a few shillings she would make up a few children's bonnets, and my sister Florrie and I would go to any neighbour who had children and try to sell them. Very often I would come home from school and there was nothing to eat until one of us effected a sale.

Once, I remember, Mum told me I would have to have the morning off from school and go to Wilmer Gardens and ask Mrs Johnson, an old friend of hers, if she would like to buy a bonnet for her eldest girl. I got there about nine-thirty in the morning, walked in and went upstairs. Being tenements, anyone could walk in.

I knocked on the door and Mrs Johnson told me to come in. I shall never forget the sight that met my eyes. There was no furniture of any sort in the room, just a tea chest and an orange box. A few wooden embers were on their last in the grate. She looked like a skeleton and was trying to feed her baby on the breast. On the tea chest was a cup of watery tea and she was crying. The sight of Mrs Johnson has never been out of my memory. Between tears, she

asked me what I wanted. I told her Mum had sent me to see if she
would like to buy a bonnet for one and threepence. The poor
woman was starving. It seemed Mr Johnson was 'inside' and the
Broker's Men had been in and stripped the place of everything in
order to get the rent that was owing. There wasn't a thing left.

This was at a time when England had the greatest empire the
world had ever known, yet most of the working population were
living below workhouse level.

Gerry duly appeared at Old Street and Mary had been advised to
attend. After hearing the case, the magistrate told him that his criminal activities must be curbed and that a stiff prison sentence was
the only way of teaching him a lesson. My sister told the magistrate
he was a good husband and pleaded that, being his first offence,
he should treat him with leniency. The beak saw my sister was due
to have a baby and told Gerry that it was due to his wife that the
original sentence he was going to impose (six months) would be cut
to three months. Poor Mary was heartbroken. Mum and Florrie were
crying when they got home. Mum told Mary she would try and see
her through until Gerry was released and the time would soon pass.
What a tower of strength my mother was! There was no help from
my father; he carried on in his drunken way and had no feeling for
any of us. To us, the children, he somehow didn't exist. We seldom
saw him. It was only at weekends that his presence was felt. He
would start on us over something trivial and we would go and stand
round Mum. We knew we were safe when she was around.

The following weeks were very bad for us all. We were behind
with the rent and saw no way of paying up. One Friday dinnertime,
a loud knock on the door sent me running to open it. A huge man
was standing there.

'Is your mother in?' he asked.

Before I could call Mum he was in. He announced he was taking
over until the rent was paid. He was the dreaded Broker's Man.

Poor Mum. She burst into tears. She just did not know where
to turn. The man took up his position in an armchair and again

emphasised the point that he would remain until the rent was forth-coming. This was the second time in my young life that I had seen the Broker's Man. The first time they took everything we had except bedding. Mum did not want this to happen again. We could only wait until the old man came home. Being Friday night, this was about seven o'clock. Mum explained what had happened but all he said was, 'I've got no bloody money, let them take the home if they want to,' and walked out. What a man.

Mum sent Florrie to my grandmother to try and borrow some money. Grandma used to teach the violin and piano and wasn't too badly off. She came back with Florrie and paid the Broker's Man off. Mum's people were fairly well off, but wouldn't have much to do with us owing to my father. If she would leave him, they were pre-pared to help in any way, but not while she stayed with him.

We now had to consider moving again. Mum saw a large flat in Rotherfield Street, Essex Road, but the snag was there was not enough room for us all. The rent was only six shillings a week and Mum couldn't miss it, so she suggested Mary should try to get a couple of rooms somewhere. She could then make a fresh start with Gerry when he was released. Mary thought this was a good idea because she did not want Gerry to meet my father when he came home. She found two rooms in a small turning off the Southgate Road. So once again we got the barrow and like nomads we were on the move again.

Our new abode was Ebenezer Buildings, Rotherfield Street. What a dump it was after the nice little house we had just left. It was a basement flat with one large room at the front and two bedrooms at the back. We soon settled in; it was a case of having to. Mary moved at the same time, but she didn't fancy sleeping on her own at first. Some nights she would pack in with us. After a while, she had to get used to the idea of going home to sleep; we hardly had enough room for ourselves. When she started to go to her own place she insisted on me going with her. I used to like that. It was nice and quiet and she used to make a fuss of me. In the mornings she would wake me up with a cup of tea and give me a breakfast with whatever she could muster, then off I'd go to school and Mary would go to Mum.

Florrie was working in a factory off the Southgate Road making Christmas crackers and she earned about ten shillings a week. She would say to me on Friday mornings, 'Meet me tonight and I'll take you to Manze's.'

On Friday night I would be outside the factory gate. Out would come Florrie, take my hand and off we would go to Manze's. This was an eel and pie shop in Hoxton Street. Florrie would go up to the counter and ask for a 'pie and half' twice. This was a meat pie and mashed potatoes with gravy. They cost three-ha'pence each. I felt on top of the world and would sit among the grown-ups and enjoy every mouthful. If Florrie could afford it, we would finish up with a fruit pie for a penny. She was a good sort. After the 'nosh up' we would go home. Florrie would give Mum her money and start on the housework.

The old man was still coming home drunk. Weekends were the worst. One Sunday night, we were all home and the old man came in paralytic drunk. He tried to get his boots off and somehow a bag of silver fell out of his pocket.

'That's not my bloody money,' he said, 'it's Peggy's.' Peggy was his foreman.

We all knew different. To make it look right, he asked Florrie to count it to make sure it was all correct. He said Florrie was the only one he could trust. Florrie proceeded to count. Every now and then she would slip two shillings or half-a-crown in her apron. After the count he told her to tie it up as he 'had to pay it in the morning'. When he went to bed Florrie passed over to Mum anything she'd managed to knock off. This sort of thing happened on several occasions. We always had a good feed the next day.

These were the days of half-sovereigns. One day Mum told me to get a threepenny bottle of gold paint. I asked her what she wanted it for and she told me 'never you mind and hurry up'. That night my father came home drunk as usual. He never hung about. He always went off to bed. Drunk as he was, he always had enough sense to slip his money bag under his side of the mattress. When all was quiet Mum slipped in to see if he had 'gone off'. When she was sure he was asleep she slipped her hand gently under the mattress and withdrew the bag. She then had to work fast in case he woke up. Out came half a sovereign, in went a painted sixpence. She would then creep in the bedroom and slip the bag back. The amazing thing about all this was we never heard another word about it.

Time was getting close for Gerry's release from prison. It was also near time for Mary's baby to be born. If the baby came before Gerry's release she was going to have it at our place. If Gerry came out first she would have it at home and Mum would look after her. The old man forbade Mary to bring Gerry to our home. He wasn't going to have any bleeding thieves in his house.

Gerry was released before the baby was born. The morning he came out the poor chap just did not know what to do. He didn't want to face the old man, knowing there would be trouble, so he walked the streets for some time, waiting for him to go to work.

About half past seven we heard stones being thrown up at the window. When Mum got up she saw Gerry standing outside. She immediately let him in, made him some tea and gave him something to eat. From his pocket he took out a small brown loaf, which was like a brick. It seems in those days the prisoners were given them on release. It was a tearful reunion. He promised Mum he would never do anything wrong again and, given a chance, he would make good.

Some time during that day Mary and Gerry went back to their own place as they didn't want any trouble with the old man. When he came home, Mum told him that Gerry was home, and threatened to 'brain him' if he started any trouble. He did eventually see Gerry, but both trod very warily. Gerry tried several ways to get a living and things were tough for him. He chopped and sold firewood, and tried 'Ragging' but wasn't very successful. Eventually, his stepfather got him a job as a fish fryer with him in a shop at London Fields. Mary's baby was born and was named after my sister Florrie. She was a sweet little thing and we all loved her very much.

Meanwhile, things were catching up with my father. He was beginning to suffer from gout and was having days off from work. This didn't help him at all and his mates were losing out. If he didn't go to work they could not operate the swindles they were working on deliveries.

The shop Gerry worked at was a large wet and dry fish shop owned and run by a Jewish family. Gerry worked well under his stepfather's supervision. He also got friendly with the owner's son, who had been a bit of a villain in his time but was now kept on a tight rein by his parents. One day while they were cleaning and cutting fish, Harry the son was telling Gerry how he would like to get his hands on some of the takings that were going into the till. The trouble was, he said, that he needed help and there had been no one he could trust. If he could find someone he could make it worth everyone's while. Gerry asked him what scheme he had in mind and he explained.

When the shop was busy, the accomplice was to come in the shop as an ordinary customer and ask for ha'penny worth of chips. But he must wait to be served by Harry, who would then serve the chips, at the same time dropping two shillings or a half-crown into the paper. The accomplice would then depart, walk down the alley at the side, sort out the money from the chips and be prepared to come in again. This would go on all night until a signal from Harry told him to go home. The money would then be collected by Gerry and shared out. The question was, who could they trust to carry out the scheme?

Gerry told Mary of Harry's scheme and she also thought it a good one. Mary approached Mum and told her all about it and wondered if she would allow me to be the accomplice. Mum told her in no mean way that she would not allow her boy to be mixed up in Gerry's bloody swindles. The schemers were now despondent, and another approach was made to Mum. Fish and chips were suggested instead of chips alone.

In the end Mum let me go, but 'Gawd help the sods if the boy gets in any trouble'. I expect Mum was thinking of the fish and chip meals I would be bringing home. I was about nine years old at the time and knew enough about life to know what I was doing.

On the appointed day to start, I went home with Mary and got introduced to Harry. He looked a real villain. He convinced me I had nothing to worry about and I would get a treat at the end of each week.

Next night I started. I was given some coppers to buy the fish and chips. When the shop got busy, in I went. I could hardly reach the counter and Harry had a job to see me among the customers.

When he spotted me he'd say, 'Yes, sonny?'

I'd say, 'Ha'penny and ha'porth', get my fish and chips, walk out, sort out the money from the fish and chips and then proceed to eat them if I was hungry, which I nearly always was. I would do this several times each night, taking great care not to let Harry's mother see me too often. I also carried a bag in my pocket for the fish and chips that I couldn't eat.

When I was given the signal 'go home' I would call in at Mary's and give her the money. She would then see me home. When I arrived they would all raid me. Saturday came and I was given sixpence or a shilling. This didn't work much of a financial proposition for me, but I stuck it out as the fish and chips helped out at home. After a few weeks Gerry told me I wasn't to go any more. It seemed that a drastic drop in the takings had taken place and Harry was suspected. So ended a big deal.

Mary and Gerry continued to see us, taking care not to see too much of the old man. Little Florrie was getting on fine. She was developing into a lovely baby and we all loved her very much; even the old man was beginning to take notice of her.

By this time, my eldest brother Will was on his way to Australia where he was to stay for two years. Before leaving he had asked Mum if his young lady could stay with us for a few days. We scarcely had room for ourselves, let alone another grown-up, but Mum hadn't liked to refuse so she wrote to the girl explaining the position. Unfortunately, however, the young lady wrote back saying that she so wanted to see us all that she just did not mind about sleeping, as anywhere would suit her. Before we knew what day it was her trunk had arrived and Nancy followed. She intended, by the look of things, to make it a permanent stay. She had been in service at Surbiton and had packed up and was going to take pot-luck with us. Goodness knows what my brother had told her. She must have thought we were better off than we were. She shared Florrie's bed and seemed a jolly sort of girl. She helped out with the chores, but had no income of any kind. She stayed for a few weeks and then started to date different men. Mum didn't like this and had to tell her to go. As far as I can remember nothing more was ever heard of her. So much for Nancy.

My brother Bert was getting himself in trouble with the police. He got caught with two other lads busting into someone's house. He came home from the 'burglary' with two tame mice and a pair of eye-glasses! This was too much for Mum and she explained to the Court that she was making application to get him away on a training ship. He got off on condition he went away. The old man and Mum had to take him to the City, I think it was Clarke Place, Bishopsgate. He was accepted for training on the *Warspite* at Greenhithe, Kent. After a few days they sent for him. We were all in tears when he went, but Mum held back hers. She had to make us see it was for his own good that he went. We heard from him after a few days and all felt better. He made the best of it and after a while he learned to become a drummer. I always remember him coming to London to play in the *Warspite* band for the Lord Mayor's Show. He was also a brilliant swimmer and won several prizes and medals. Mum was certainly right to send him away. God knows how he would have finished up if she hadn't.

On more than one occasion I had to stay away from school because I had no boots. The terrible part of all this was my father who was still coming home the worse for drink and had money in his pocket (though how much of it had been honestly come by I do not know).

One day I took a note to school asking the teacher to excuse my absence the previous day, due to the rain and the fact that I had no serviceable boots. The teacher must have had a word with one of the better-off boys and next morning I was called out of class. He took me to the lobby and asked me to try on an old pair of boots. I knew the boy who had given them and wished the ground would open and swallow me up. Every time I saw that boy I had the feeling he was telling his mates I was wearing his boots.

My sister Florrie made life as happy as she could for my young sister Amelia and myself. Sometimes on a Monday night she would come home from work and if she had a few coppers left over from the weekend she would say to Mum, 'Get yourself and the kids ready, we're going up the Brit.' This was the old Britannia Theatre in Hoxton. Florrie loved the dramas that were performed there. If Mum could afford it we had a bag of peanuts or a ha'penny bag of sweets. We went in the 'gallery' for twopence – half price for us kids. Among the dramas I remember was *The Face at the Window* – real horrible. Others were *Sweeney Todd, Maria Marten, Why Girls Leave Home.* Many times I have lain awake after going to the Brit, terrified to open my eyes for fear of seeing the murdered lying next to me.

Sometimes we went to Collins Music Hall or the Islington Empire. That was different. They always had variety shows. We saw Harry Champion, Vesta Tilley, The Two Bobs, Hetty King, comedians of all sorts and stars of the day. We always dreaded coming home after these outings. The old man would start a row as soon as we entered the door. He thought Mum should always be at his beck and call. Florrie got to the age when she would stand no nonsense from him. As soon as he started to create she would stand up to him and defy him to touch any one of us. He was a crafty old devil and knew how far to go. Mum had a good ally in Florrie.

About February 1914 he had an accident at work. He cut the top of his finger off and had to stay at home. No money was forthcoming, not that he ever gave us much. Six or seven shillings was the most he ever gave Mum. Now she also had to keep him, so to help out she got herself a job making ladies' coats. Before she went out in the morning she left him some money to get dinners for us children. All we ever had from him was bread and marge or bread and jam. The rest of the money he'd spend at the local pub.

One night she asked us what we had had for dinner and one of us told her. She nearly went mad. When he came home that night he got the biggest hiding a woman could possibly give a man. But he was no man. She called him all the 'starving gits' she could lay her tongue to. (That was a favourite word of Mum's when she was angry.)

She wouldn't go back to work after that. She explained to the firm what had happened and they gave her some work to do at home. She would save all the cloth cuttings and when things got really bad and she had no money I would be detailed to take them to a rag shop in St John's Road and see how much I could get for them. She sorted the woollens from the cottons and I got more for them that way than I would have if they had been mixed. If the old boy was in a good mood I would get sixpence or eightpence. I was then instructed to 'go down Hoxton' and get 6 lb of potatoes, 1 lb onions and 1 ½ lb of 'back fat'. This would come to about fivepence. Mum would then cut the fat into small pieces and fry it, mash up the potatoes, pour the fat in the middle and mix the lot up. Small pieces of onion would then be fried brown and these she would mix in also. We would then have a plateful each and we really felt we had had something to eat.

We often used to say to Mum, 'When are we going to have a mixed dinner, Mum?'

Her reply would be, 'See how much money we have when you come out from school.' If there was no money it would be bread and jam. The old man eventually went back to work and spent what compensation money he got on drink.

About this time we had a visit from Gerry who came in one night frantic with worry. He told Mum little Florrie had got pneumonia and was in a bad way. Could she go back with him at once? Mum wouldn't leave my sister Amelia and I so we all went home with Gerry. The old man cut up rough about us all going. Mum called him a wicked and selfish old sod to talk like that on such a sad occasion.

When we got to Mary's, Gerry had to go back to work. The fish shop was open to midnight and he had to be there to clean up. Poor little Florrie was in a bad way and the doctor didn't hold out much hope. Mary, Mum and Florrie were crying, and Mary begged us not to leave her. Arrangements were made to stop the night. My sister and I were put to bed while all the others slept in chairs. But there was no sleep for anyone. Little Florrie died during the night. Their eyes were red with crying and loss of sleep. Mum pulled everyone together and we all went back to our place. Gerry was left to make arrangements with the local undertaker. I am sure little Florrie was not insured. Gerry had to appeal to the boss's son Harry to help him out, which he did. After the funeral Mary and Gerry moved to a flat in Hackney Road. The place they had gave too many memories of the baby.

Towards the summer of 1914 Nemesis was catching up with the old man. He had the gout really badly and could not go to work. He had to stay in bed for six weeks. He had never been so ill. Mum had to struggle again. It was purgatory for the old man to stay in bed. He couldn't drink and he was afraid of losing his job. He had need to be worried. They gave someone else the job of delivering goods and it didn't take the chap long to see what was going on. He blew the gaff to the boss and all who had been concerned got the sack. He was well and truly worried when his partners in crime called in and told him what had happened.

The firm hadn't made up their minds about prosecution. He told Mum that when he was able to get up he might have to go to prison. Her words to him were, 'Serve you bloody well right. The biggest rogue gets caught in the end.' He got no sympathy from Mum. His panel money had been delayed and when it did come through Mum asked the insurance man if he could let her have it. He said he couldn't do that, as the old man had to sign for it. It was about £4. He went in the bedroom to see him, paid him and went.

Mum went in after and asked the old man, 'What about it?'

'What about what?' he said.

'The bloody insurance money,' said Mum.

'He only gave me fifteen shillings,' said the old man, 'the other's not come through yet.'

She called him all the old tykes and rotters she could think of, but it was no use. He would not part up. She managed to get four shillings or five shillings out of him and had to let it go at that.

He was now staked and wanted a drink. He called me in his bedroom and told me to get him 'a quart of ale and hurry up'. I was not old enough to go inside the pub, so the procedure was to wait outside and when someone went in to ask them if they would please get the beer. I had done this on several occasions. This particular night I got the beer in a quart can with a wire handle. Going home I would swing the can, that was now full up, a full circle the length of my arm. This I had done several times and was now an expert, or thought I was.

I was merrily swinging the beer when suddenly the handle parted company from the can and the beer went in the road. I was petrified with fear at what the old man would do to me when I got home. When I arrived I told Mum what had happened.

'A bloody good job,' she said.

'But how am I going to tell him?' I asked.

'Come with me,' she said, and in we went. When she told him what had happened his face went purple. He called me all the 'daft bleeders' he could think of.

'Serves you bloody well right, you shouldn't send a child for beer,' said Mum.

I thanked God that he couldn't get up. Anyhow, he got his beer in the end. Florrie went to save the peace.

One night during that week, when we had all gone to bed, there was a terrific scuffle in the road. The old man just could not keep his nose out of a fight; it somehow fascinated him. He woke Mum up and said, 'Ann, there ain't half a bloody fight going on outside.'

Half asleep, she replied, 'Mind your own business and go to sleep, it's nothing to do with you.'

Although he could hardly move, he somehow managed to get himself to the street door and stood there in his pants and socks for quite a while. While he was watching the fight, Mum went to turn over and to get to sleep, when she felt her leg touch something. She grabbed it and when she looked it was the old man's panel money. He had hidden it in his sock and it fell out when he got up. Mum immediately tumbled what it was and hid it in her nightdress. After the fight the old man got back to bed and off to sleep.

Next morning Mum got up and gave him a cup of tea. As she got near the door she saw him through the crack looking all over the bed.

'Have you lost something?' said Mum.

'Don't look so bloody innocent,' said the old man, 'you know what I've lost.'

'How should I know?' said Mum.

'I had a few bob left out of my panel money and if it's not here you've bleeding well pinched it,' was the old man's comment.

'Where did you keep it?' said Mum.

'In me bloody sock,' said the old man and he was blue in the face.

'Well,' said Mum, 'you shouldn't have poked your nose into that fight last night. If it's lost, you lost it then.'

He had us look all over the place for it. What a time Mum gave us next day! I had new boots, Amelia new shoes and Florrie wasn't forgotten either. The old man never would say how much he lost.

As he got better he would somehow manage to get to the local pub. He still had his panel money coming in. In the end that got stopped. A Health Visitor called one night and he was out. That was his lot. The Visitor's report went in and they stopped his money. He now had to think about a job. He still reckoned his firm owed him a week's wages. He wrote out a note asking his foreman to pay his son any money due to him and told me to come with him to deliver the note. I remember the road but not the name of the firm. We walked to Danbury Street, Islington. We got to the place and he told me to go through a wicket gate, ask for the foreman and deliver the note. I had instructions that should the foreman ask where he was, I was to say he was ill in bed. He retired out of sight with hopes running high.

I went in the gate, asked for the foreman and gave him the note. I waited quite a while for a reply. The foreman eventually came out and gave me twopence and told me to mind the road going home and give this note to Dad. I found the old man and gave him the note. He read it and was livid. He never said a word to me. When I got home, Mum asked me if I got the old man's money. I told her about the letter. He still hadn't told Mum the contents. She found the letter eventually in his pocket. It was worded to the effect that they had thought the matter over and if it wasn't for his having a wife and children he would have had to answer to the law for his thieving in the past, and they warned him never to show himself near the firm again.

He now had to get himself a job. The First World War had broken out and things were looking grim. All Mum's friends were calling in, crying that their husbands had been called up from the reserves. They all came to us with their troubles.

The only job the old man could find was in a timber mill at King's Cross. Now he really knew what work was all about! He used to come home with his shoulders raw from humping timber. This didn't stop him from boozing. He kept all his money, but he had to go easy during the week as he only had what he earned and no longer had any chance of fiddling.

When he was young he had belonged to the Volunteers – some form of Territorial Army – with a good excuse to go drinking. He had a framed certificate on the wall to the effect that he had passed his drill instruction. He was always boasting to people that if it wasn't for us he would 'join up tomorrow'. The times I've heard him arguing with people as to how the war should be fought and won. His point of argument was 'there was no force in the world that could beat a British square'. He just wasn't capable of thinking beyond the Zulu War.

One Saturday night, half cut as usual, he was boasting how he would 'join up tomorrow if it wasn't for his commitments'. Mum overheard him and asked what he considered his commitments.

'Surely you can leave the pub, which is the only commitment I know you have.'

She also called him a coward and told him in no uncertain words that 'he didn't have the guts of a louse'.

'Am I?' he said. 'Stan,' meaning me, 'write this letter as I tell you.' Being anxious for him to go, I got paper and pen and wrote as he dictated. I even took his certificate from the Volunteers and enclosed that with the letter and sent it to Whitehall. He knew they wouldn't have him. Back came a letter saying he was too old. We were all disappointed.

One morning Mary and Gerry's mother called. They were both crying. Unbeknown to them he had packed in his job at the fish shop and joined up. He was called up that morning.

CHAPTER THREE

Gerry joining up was a shock to us in every way. He had always been against the army. No bloody army would get him, he would say. I think his job in the fish shop was the reason. He worked very long hours; nine o'clock in the morning, home again at three o'clock, on again at five o'clock and there he was until midnight. Joining the army was an escape for him.

This had now put Mum in a spot. Mary would not stay on her own after losing little Florrie. She just could not settle down. We hardly had enough room for ourselves, so Mum suggested we try for another place to live and all be together. Flats were not large enough for us all. One afternoon, Mum and Mary went house-hunting. After looking at several, they decided on a house in Loanda Street – Number 15. This was a small house by the side of the Regent's Canal near the bridge in Kingsland Road. By taking this house we had a room for Mary. They thought the war wouldn't last long and when it was over and Gerry came out of the army they could get another place of their own.

We couldn't move on a barrow this time. With Gerry and Bert away, this only left me, and I was too small to attempt it. We had to have a horse and van. In those days a noticeboard was in every greengrocer's shop stating 'Horse & Van 1 /3d. per hour'. Mum reckoned if we packed everything ourselves it would only take three to four hours, so we ordered the horse and van. It was something new for us. We must have thought we were the aristocracy after previous moves with a barrow.

We settled in at the new address and the first night we were kept awake with bugs. They came from every crack in the wallpaper. When the landlord had the place decorated they must have papered

40

over the bugs. Mum had a friend living two doors away, who suggested we got some carbolic. I went and got a 'penn'orth of carbolic' and Mum and her friend went bug-hunting. They also sealed up one room at a time and got some sulphur candles going. This kept them down, but it was a job to get rid of them altogether. In those days nearly everyone had bugs and it was usually a question of keeping them down rather than expecting to be completely free of them.

I had to change schools and went to Haggerston Road School. Of all the schools I had been to, this was the toughest, both as regards the teachers and the boys who attended. One was forever trying to keep out of trouble. I could usually hold my own with most of the boys whatever school I went to, but these were the toughest villains I ever knew. I got the measure of most of them in the end and after a fight or two, and a caning from the headmaster, I was accepted as one of them. I was also invited to go 'scrumping' for fruit down Spitalfields Market, but had to decline the offer as this could only be done during the dinner hour when I was nearly always wanted at home. In any case my mother forbade me to get mixed up with a bad crowd.

I could see the wisdom of her words. On more than one occasion a boy would be missing from school for a week or two. When he came back he'd had his hair cropped short, like an old-time convict, and we knew he had been in a Remand Home.

The old man changed his job after the move. He wasn't 'going all the soddin' way to King's Cross' so he got himself a job at a local timber yard by the name of King & Scarborough in the Kingsland Road, again humping timber. I used to sit on the wall for hours watching the men stack the timber. One day a film company set up their gear and were filming a thriller. The actors were jumping from stack to stack, and when the hero caught the villain a fight ensued and the villain got slung in the water. It was thrilling to watch.

The old man wasn't earning so much money and couldn't get as drunk as he used to. One day he suggested to Mum he would like to come home to dinner as he was so near home. He would pay Mum any extra money it cost. After the first week, however, he never kept his promise and Mum wouldn't stand for it any more. He just did not like paying out.

In order to keep things going, Mum said she would like to start a small shop. She could then make up boys' trousers, girls' frocks and pinafores, etc. After giving the matter much thought, I was told to go and get two orange boxes and two apple boxes. I took a mate with me and went down Hoxton to get the boxes. Mum said she was going to turn the front room into a shop. In those days no planning permission was needed. Between Mum and myself we made a platform and side-wings, got some wallpaper, and in no time had our shop-front. Mum made dresses, trousers and all kinds of children's wear.

When they were set out it looked very nice. Neighbours used to pay off a sixpence or a shilling, and when they paid up got the goods. This was all right but she had started to run out of materials to make clothes up with. Her sister had married a chap who owned a clothing factory in Camden Passage, Islington. He used to employ girls making dresses and coats. He was in a fair way of business. Mum went to see them and arranged to buy up all the off-cuts of material. These were triangle-shaped pieces and were in bundles. He wouldn't give them to her, but offered to sell them at so much a bundle. He was dead mean. Here was her own brother-in-law who had all the money he needed, his own two houses and servants, yet was too mean to let my mother have these without paying for them. How low my uncle was in my eyes, he'll never know!

The problem was how to get the stuff home; they were heavy. She mentioned this to the old man and it was suggested that I go once a week to collect them. I didn't know my way to Camden Passage, so the old man showed me. He took me all round the back doubles and I found it was no mean walk. I had to have something to put the bundles in. Mum gave me a few coppers and I went to the local rag shop for a pair of old pram wheels and axle, got a sugar box from the grocer at the corner and made myself a cart.

Once every week after school, Mum would get me something to eat and off I would go to Camden Passage. My uncle would take the money and give me the bundle and then I'd start to walk home. It took me the best part of three hours to get there and back. Many's the time I got soaked to the skin, but Mum did appreciate the help I was giving her.

Going to Camden Passage I would have to pass Edie's Bar. Here one could get a large cup of tea and a lump of 'Tottenham' cake for a penny. If I could get a penny before leaving I would pull up at Edie's and have a tea and cake and really enjoy it. It was a very popular place and was always crowded with poor people. The carmen used to put up there and it was so crowded that one could very seldom get a seat.

Mum's shop was taking just about enough to exist on. Sometimes she would be on the machine until midnight. It wasn't much of a life for us. Mary got herself a job at De-Leefs in Kingsland Road and when she and Florrie came home at night they had to get everything ready themselves. The old man could see Mum had a few bob coming in and he stopped giving her the six or seven shillings that he had done in the past. There were rows every weekend. He still came home drunk on Saturday and Sunday, and life was really unbearable.

Gerry was stationed at Woolwich and came home weekends if he could, but he was getting fed up. He missed his freedom. One weekend when he was planning to come home his leave got stopped. They had put him on a recruiting drive. The district he was coming to was Hoxton. He wrote a card to Mary explaining why he couldn't get home. I had heard about this drive and thought I would go and see it. He was in the Royal Horse Artillery and mounted on horseback. I was standing in Hoxton High Street when the parade came along. There was a mounted band followed by the soldiers on horseback, followed by the marching infantry. I saw Gerry on his horse and waved to him. He couldn't stop but beckoned to me. I ran alongside of him and he told me they would be stopping at Pitfield

Street later that night and to tell Mary to meet him there at a certain time. It was very important. I got the message back to Mary and she went along to find him. She came back very worried. She told Mum he was fed up with the army and he was going to desert. The old man created when he heard about it. He threatened to give him away to the police. He wasn't going to have 'any bleeding deserters' in his house.

Gerry did desert and he was on the run. The police came several times. Looking back, one can't help feeling sorry for him. One night there was a knock on the door and when I opened it there was Gerry. He ran in quick, shut the door and said, 'Is the old 'un in?' He frightened the life out of me. He was dishevelled and dirty. 'No, the old man's out,' I said.

With that, he ran upstairs to Mary and it was tragic to see them in each other's arms. The police must have been watching. They knocked a few minutes after Gerry. Gerry guessed who it was, jumped out of the back window and was away. They never caught him.

To crown all, my brother Bert came home from the *Warspite* training ship. He had finished his training and was going in the Merchant Navy. Ships were being sunk in great numbers by the Germans and none of us felt too good about it. Mum said, 'If anything happens to him, I'll never forgive myself.' She couldn't get it out of her mind that by putting him away on the *Warspite* she was somehow responsible. He didn't seem to mind and to ease her mind said he would have gone in the Merchant Navy anyway.

The police were still looking for Gerry and the word had got around to the neighbours. The boys at school had got to know and I had many a bust-up defending him.

Everything was now getting too much for Mum and she reckoned the house had a curse on it. The only way out was to move again. This time she found a house in Scawfell Street. This wasn't far from Loanda Street. It certainly looked a road with some life in it, which was what we were used to. Loanda Street was a drab place of flat-fronted houses where everyone closed their doors. There wasn't the friendliness, so we moved again with horse and van.

The new house had three rooms down and four up. It was the first house in the road and next door was a huge stable belonging to Thos. Cook & Son. Many horses and brakes were stabled there, which proved of great interest to me. There was also a small garden. Mary had the front room upstairs and lived with us. It looked as if it was going to be a happy house.

We hadn't been in long before Gerry arrived, just as if nothing had happened. The police were off his tail and he somehow seemed to have got away with it. He got himself a job and was now leading a normal life.

The old man also got himself another job. He went to see some of his old cronies around Shoreditch and got in as a timber salesman. He had a pony and trap and was doing well. He seemed in the money again, not that it made much difference to us as he still kept it to himself.

We were now well into 1915 and several commodities were in short supply. Among them were screws and glue. If any could be obtained a good price could be had from the small cabinetmakers in the district. Gerry and the old man were on friendly terms and were now going to the local to have a drink together. Evidently, during their drinking bouts, the old man told Gerry what a wonderful market there was for screws and glue and how he wished he could get hold of some. Gerry was working in Bethnal Green Road, making munition boxes. Plenty of screws and glue were used in their construction. Gerry reckoned he could get plenty but some arrangement would have to be made to collect them. He could get them out during his afternoon tea break, but not dinnertime or night-time. I was approached and asked to go each day to meet Gerry during his afternoon tea break. Mum went mad when she knew what they were up to, but between the two of them they managed to convince her there was no risk. I had to take a shopping bag to school with me and then proceed to Bethnal Green Road at four o'clock. I can't

remember the name of the pub where I had to meet Gerry. At the side of the pub there was a gents' toilet that was always open. When Gerry came along I would dive in and he would follow. He would quickly undo his apron and take out packets of screws and packets of dried glue from inside his trousers. He also had his pockets stuffed. They were quickly dropped in the bag and I would walk home. This I had to do every day of the week and Saturday mornings also. The old man would take them on his round and flog them to various small cabinetmakers. On Saturday afternoons they would share out the proceeds. I don't remember ever getting anything out of this, but I suppose I must have done. Mum wouldn't have let me do it for nothing. It's a marvel I didn't grow up a criminal the things I had to do for them.

On Saturday, Gerry and the old man, who were now the best of friends, would go drinking in a pub at the corner of Weymouth Terrace. We now had a front room again and many's the drunken parties we had. Mum would sometimes go with Mary for a drink on Saturday nights and the old man would treat them to anything they would care to drink, but he still wouldn't give her a penny for the home. Mum didn't drink much. She would have a gin and clove, and then try to get a seat near the corner. The old man would call up for drinks and often forget his change. The barman knew Mum and when this happened he would give Mum a wink and a nod and push it over towards her. She had reasons for going.

Mum decided to start selling clothes again. One Friday she said to me, 'Stan, I want you to go down Hoxton in the morning and see if you can find a site where we can pitch a stall.' The market was usually chock-a-block with stalls but this didn't deter her from sending me to have a look round. I started from the 'narrow way' of Hoxton and walked along towards Old Street, but couldn't see many vacant places. Coming back, I saw somewhere that took my eye. In the centre of the road between Nuttall Street and Wilmer Gardens were two public lavatories, flanked all round by a wide pavement. There were two or three stalls there but plenty of room for more. Home I went and told Mum. This pleased her and she thought she could do all right there, so I had to start the walk to Camden Passage again. But I had lost my cart.

Some time ago I had to go to Whiston Street Gasworks for three penn'orth of coke. To get the coke I went in the gate, paid my threepence in the office and got a ticket. I then went to where the men were filling the sacks, got loaded and went back to where I had left my cart. When I got there someone had pinched it. I should have known better. The lads round there could take your laces out of your boots and you wouldn't know they were gone. I had to carry the coke home and swore I would somehow get my cart back. Mary was expecting another baby and had bought a second-hand pram. I had to borrow the pram and push it to Camden Passage, get loaded and push it all the way home. I felt a 'Charlie' pushing that pram, but the thought of tea and cake at Edie's Bar was the carrot that kept the donkey going. Mum worked hard all that week and bought and mended any old clothes she could find and got them ready for the stall on the coming Saturday.

Opposite the house where we lived was a coal shop and they had a couple of barrows which they let out on hire. I booked one for Saturday, when at eight sharp I got it loaded up with two sacks of clothes, old boots and anything Mum thought she could sell. I pushed the barrow and Mum walked alongside of me. I was just hoping the pitch was vacant. It was and I was overjoyed.

I propped up the barrow with the front legs I had brought along with me so that Mum could sit on it. We had some boards and these we laid out on the barrow. Mum unpacked the clothes and we were away. By nine-thirty people were beginning to flock into the market and we soon had some customers. The frocks and pinafores went like wildfire. 'Fifteen pence the frocks,' Mum would say, and 'nine-pence the pinafores.'

About midday we were half sold out. I asked Mum if she would like some tea. 'Ere y'are, son,' she said, and took the money out of the takings. I got a jug of tea and some sandwiches and we ate them ravenously. We'd had no breakfast owing to our having to start out early. Three o'clock came and we had sold out. Mum told me to stay with the barrow while she went shopping, and came back loaded. She treated me to the pictures and gave me money to buy sweets. I had never known such times.

Florrie was working in a factory at Shoreditch, also making munition boxes. The work was hard and it didn't seem to agree with her. Several times she went to the doctor who advised her to change her job, but she still carried on.

Mum was now working harder in order to keep the stall going. I was still going to my uncle's to get the cuttings, and Mum also visited the local 'Tot Shops' to see if she could buy up any second-hand bits that she could earn a few bob on. If old boots had holes in them, we'd mend them. I had some boot-repairing experience. The school used to run a boot-repair class. After school, one could take a penny and the instructor would show us how to repair our boots with pieces of leather. I could only do one in the time allowed, so if both were worn out I would have to go to school the next day with one boot sound and the other with a hole that could not be mended until the evening.

Twenty minutes or so before the class closed there was a panic. Most of us couldn't finish in time and the instructor would work like a Trojan finishing our boots since very few of us owned a spare pair. Mum gave me the money to buy a 'hobbin foot' and for one and threepence I got a foot and post and set about mending the boots. They always sold for a few coppers.

We took the stuff out every week and did fairly well. Sometimes, after getting Mum set up, I would go for a walk looking at the shops. Opposite our stall was 'The Land of Promise', as it was called. This was the local workhouse. It was a heart-rending sight to see the old people through the gates. I can never forget it. After a lifetime of hard work these poor old people were left destitute and finished up in this horrible place. Husbands and wives were separated and on Thursdays and Sundays were let out for a few hours. The husband was usually first out and would wait at the gates for his wife. It was heartbreaking to see them embrace each other. The poor old souls were dressed in workhouse fashion. The men had a hard grey suit, cap and heavy boots. The old ladies wore a long skirt and cape with a bonnet that tied under the chin, also all in grey. They would take each other by the arm and walk away, perhaps to relations or the local park.

I have said that next door to our house were the stables of Thos. Cook. In the summer the brakes would leave each morning taking the women from the clubs or pubs on a day's outing. They would start off about eight-thirty in the morning for Chingford, Loughton or Theydon Bois in rural Essex. Each brake was pulled by two or three horses and held about twenty-four people. A man or lad stood on the back to keep the urchins off. One of my schoolmates had been out on this trip, as brake-boy, and told me what a good day out it was. The driver had bought his food and given him half the collection, given by the trippers, who were nearly always half-cut coming home. I thought I would like to do this, so I asked Mum if I could have a day off from school and go. She had a word with the driver, who told her I would be all right and I would be looked after, so she agreed.

On the Monday morning I was up bright and early and waited for the brake to come out of the yard.

'Jump on,' said the driver, and away we went.

The first of my troubles started as we got round the corner. I saw a load of my class-mates and they were shouting and threatening to tell my teacher where I was. When we picked up the women and they were all in, I squashed my leg in the door, which made tears come to my eyes. All in all I wasn't doing so good. By the time we got to Theydon Bois I wasn't feeling at all happy. The driver didn't give me much to eat and I was really miserable. They started for home about seven o'clock and by the time they had stopped at various pubs, time was getting on. After the last call they passed round the hat, gave the driver the money and I got home about eleven o'clock. The driver gave me sixpence, wished me good night and indoors I went. When I got in, Mum and Florrie were frantic.

'Where have you been all this time?' asked Mum.

I told her I could only get home as fast as the horses would bring me and it was no fault of mine if I was late. I also told her I was hungry and she nearly went mad to think I had hardly had anything to eat all day. While she was getting me something ready she asked me how much the driver had given me. When I said sixpence, that done it.

'Come with me, Florrie,' she said to my sister, 'no bugger is going to take liberties with my boy.' Down to the stables they went. They asked for the driver, whose name was Tich, went among the horses and found him and gave him hell for leather. He had to give me another half-crown and nearly got done-up in the bargain. It was the last brake ride I ever had.

CHAPTER FOUR

Gerry and the old man were still doing well and on Saturday nights they used to celebrate often. Some of their mates were coming home on leave from the trenches, some were covered in mud, and their first stop was the pub nearest to where they lived. Back home they would come with a load of beer and a party was soon in full swing. This usually ended up in a free fight. The old man was always in the thick of it. He'd take up his usual place on the stairs and challenge anyone. He and Gerry were always at it, yet on Sunday morning they'd be the best of pals.

'Coming for a drink, Bill?' Gerry would say.

'Coming now, mate,' the old man would reply, and off they would go as if they had never had a bad word. By dinnertime they had had enough.

Every Sunday dinnertime the old man would come home half-cut and then wait for his dinner. On one occasion he took his coat off and sat by the fire. Mum got the joint out of the oven and started to cut it. Florrie was seeing to the vegetables. He'd been nagging all the time he sat there and as Mum started to cut the meat he must have felt hungry.

'I'll have the first cut,' he said.

She gave him one smack with the back of her hand right round his chops.

'Take that. I'll give you first bloody cut,' and with that the force of the clout knocked him in the fireplace. We all started to laugh It was the most comical sight to see. He went for Florrie because he saw her laughing, and she gave him one. He finished up with nothing and went to bed. This was the sort of thing we had to put up with every Sunday dinnertime. How my mother stuck it out all those years I never know. I have been trying to find the answer to that one for years but haven't found it so far.

Early one morning I was awakened by a baby crying. Mary had given birth to a baby boy. Mum and Florrie had been up all night and were looking very tired. He was a nice little chap and I spent many hours looking after him and taking him out in his pram. After Mary got well she bought herself a sewing machine and started taking in homework. Twice a week I had to go to Golden Lane and get a bundle of bandoliers. They were all cut ready for making. It seemed I was now at everyone's beck and call. It was 'Stan go here', 'Stan go there'. I hardly got time to play in the street. Mum reckoned the boys were too rough and I always had to be near in case I was wanted. Some of the lads weren't too bad. Once they knew you could look after yourself if they come any rough stuff, you were accepted. I was invited many times to join them in their street fights, but managed to steer clear. I always had something to do or somewhere to go.

These street fights were not funny. A boy would have a fight at school. If he got a pasting, he and his mates would find out where the other boy lived. They would then get together and come *en masse* loaded with bricks, stones or anything they could lay their hands on. Sometimes the other side got wind of what was happening and they would meet them loaded with all sorts of implements. Heads got cut and windows broken. Sometimes the police would be called and a retreat in all directions would take place. Street fights were not for me.

About this time, 1916, Mum was getting worried. She hadn't heard from my brothers and many ships were being sunk. One day Mum and Florrie went to the Admiralty to see why we had heard nothing from my eldest brother. They assured her that all was well.

We were having Zeppelin raids also. Mum wouldn't let us go to bed too early and in the summer we would all sit on the coping at the side of the house where all the neighbours would also congregate; it helped to pass the time. The old man bought himself a bottle of *Liquid Sunshine* rum. He said it would come in handy in case anyone felt queer during an air raid.

One Saturday night he came home half-cut and the warning went. Police would come round with a card on their chest which said 'Take Cover' and blow their whistles. We all went to the door to see what was happening when, suddenly, a gun went off. The old man shot upstairs for his rum. He came tearing down again and wanted to know who had pinched his 'bleeding rum'.

'You'll leave it alone,' said Mum. She had hidden it. He was blowing his top. He reckoned he was feeling ill and in the end she had to give it to him. Every time a bang went he had a drop more rum. Suddenly in the sky we saw a small red glow which gradually got bigger. It was a Zeppelin coming down in flames. Everyone cheered and the old man celebrated by drinking all his rum. So much for his concern for anyone who might feel queer in a later raid!

Next morning we read the Zeppelin had been shot down by Lt. Robinson and had landed at Cuffley, in Hertfordshire.

Some nights the lads would sit on the coping and start singing and wake up Mary's baby. Mum would ask them to clear off. They usually went without comment. One night they were singing alto and treble at the top of their voices and Mum asked them to go. They wouldn't move. She lost all patience in the end and got a big jug of water and slung the lot out of the window. It drenched the lot. The look on their faces was one of amazement and disgust.

'Aw, Mrs J, you didn't ought to have done that,' they said.

'Serves you bloody well right,' said Mum, 'and if you start again tomorrow night you'll get some more.'

I think they had a lot of respect for her after that. She only had to open the window if they started anything and they would shut up like clams. She thought the world of those lads really and often used to ask them in for a cup of tea. They always knew where they stood with her.

About this time, my young sister Amelia was starting school. I used to take her to the gate and Mum would meet her at twelve o'clock. I was still at the same school and the masters and teachers were tyrants in my eyes. Looking back, they had something to put up with. They had to be tough to survive. I am sure the discipline they dished out did us the world of good in later years.

We still had our stall in Hoxton, and I used to sit on a box and watch the women shopping. In those days they were treated by their menfolk like serfs. Most of them were dressed in a long skirt and a coarse canvas apron, with an old coat or shawl over their shoulders and a man's cap with a big hatpin on their heads. All their shopping was put in their aprons. Usually there were two or three children tagging along. Somehow they didn't seem to know anything different. Most of them came from poverty-stricken homes and drink was a common cause for misery as well as an escape from it. It needed a strong character like our mum to keep on an even keel.

Mary decided to have the baby christened. She named him after Gerry. On the Sunday she gave a party. It was the usual beer-up. The old man and Gerry dressed up as women and went to the pub like it. They were singing and dancing in the bar and really going to town. They all returned home and went up to Mary's and Gerry's to finish the celebration. They sang and danced and all the ornaments started to fall off the wall. If ever the floor nearly fell in, it did that night. And by way of a change there were no fights. Neighbours couldn't believe it.

The old man was beginning to get the gout again and had to have a few days off. They gave his round to another chap, who called in to see how he was. He just couldn't make out why the pony stopped at every pub. He didn't know my father.

About six o'clock one night I thought I saw a boy with my cart, the one that had been pinched at the Gas Works. I challenged him and he denied it. I went and got Gerry to prove it was mine. Gerry was prepared to give the boy the benefit of the doubt but I knew it was mine. Gerry went indoors again and he was never the same chap in my eyes after that. I was prepared to fight for it, and I did. We were fighting in the middle of the road and I was getting the best of it when a taxi nearly run us over and stopped outside our house. Who should get out but my brother Bert and a mate. I ran up to him and he put his arms round me like elder brothers do. I was too dazed to do anything about my cart. I just remember the boy getting up and running off with it.

My brother's homecoming boosted our morale. It was such a long time since we had seen him. I remember running upstairs and shouting, 'Mum, Bert's home.' She was on the machine at the time and thought I was kidding until he came in. She kissed and cuddled him and could hardly believe it. His mate was much older than my brother. I'd say he was about thirty-five and he was a French Canadian. Tall and broad with a Clark Gable moustache. He could hardly speak English but he made himself understood.

We had a real reunion. My brother looked a lot older and was well tanned. He had been on tankers out East. Mum and Florrie rushed around and got them a meal and after they went to the local for a drink. Everyone went: Gerry, Mary, Florrie and Mum. Needless to say they met the old man. It was a grand slam and everyone came back home. Bert's mate was named Max. He saw the old man liked rum and bought him a bottle. I was sent to the local fish shop and ordered fish and chips galore. They had money to burn. After a glorious beer-up, and listening to their adventures, it was very late when the party packed up. Max went back to the Sailors' Home somewhere in docklands and was invited to come again tomorrow.

Next morning, I was told not to go to school as I had some errands to do. Bert had quite a bit of money and gave Mum several pounds. I soon discovered what errands I had to get.

'Get the pram and go to the pawnshop,' said Mum. My mother always seemed to have a stack of pawn tickets; she reckoned she could play cards with them. I got the pram and Mum gave me a load of tickets and away I went to McCarthys, a pawnshop in Great Cambridge Street. When I went in with the stack of tickets the chap behind the counter asked me if we had come into a fortune.

Anyhow, I got the pram loaded and got them home. There were sheets, costumes, suits and all sorts of goods Mum never knew she had.

Bert said he wasn't home for long and had to see about 'signing on'. Max came during the day and they went to a shipping office to see about their next trip. They came back and said their ship was sailing in about four days, so they were prepared to have a spending spree. During the next four days they painted the Hackney Road red. The old man didn't go to work; he wasn't going to be left out. He was so drunk that he was helpless most of the time. I remember on one occasion he had to be put to bed and he thought he was dying. He was shouting for me in his drunken stupor. I didn't want to go as I had seen him like this before. Mum told me to 'go and see what he wants'. I went in the bedroom and he told me to come nearer and hold his hand.

'Stan, I don't think I'm long for this world,' he said, and made me promise to look after my mother. I was the 'only one he could trust' and on and on he went. I stayed with him until he gradually went to sleep, and crept out of the room. I told my mother what he had said and she told me 'not to worry, he'll be about again as soon as the drink wears off'. True enough he was and he didn't remember a thing about it.

Bert and Max went back when the four days were up and promised to be back in six weeks. They were both well and truly broke. So we were back to normal again. Going to Camden Passage for the cloth, putting the stall out on Saturday; nothing had changed. Going to meet Gerry and bringing back the screws and glue. The continual drunken rows at weekends. I was beginning to wish I was old enough to be able to get away from it all.

I got friendly with a boy who lived at the top end of Scawfell Street, this was the 'upper ten'. No one would play with this boy. All the 'herbs' thought he was a snob. His name was David Pugh. He was Welsh. His father worked in the City and was very strict in the Welsh way of life.

One day I was invited to have tea with them. Dave said it was all right as he'd asked his mum. I didn't want to go as I thought it was a bit out of my class. He managed to get me to go in the end. His mother was typically Welsh. I could hardly understand her. He also had two older sisters. I'll never forget sitting down to tea. It was all so different to what I was used to. Luckily I was always taught good manners by my mother and it came in handy on this occasion. I was given the choice of white or brown bread, real butter and jam, cakes and everything. After tea, Dave and his father asked me out in the garden and we played games. I began to wonder why my father was so different. I didn't know fathers played with their children. Anyhow, although it was out of my class, I enjoyed it and thanked them for having me. I was told I could come again.

Dave and I were always together. We were staunch pals. When we came out of school we used to go for walks to the City. The trouble was I always had to go somewhere or do something. When I had to meet Gerry I used to run all the way to Bethnal Green Road and back. I couldn't tell Dave what I was up to so I made excuses that I'd be late and would see him later. It was the same when I had to go to my uncle's at Camden Passage.

Dave's family were very religious and were firm supporters of Lloyd George. I didn't mind their politics but could not see eye to eye with their religion. I had seen too much poverty and suffering to have many religious thoughts. We used to argue our points on this but never let it interfere with our friendship. My mother approved of us being friends and on occasions would tell me to bring Dave to tea. We did the best we could, but could not put on a show like Dave's mother. Again, if ever he was at our place, I was always afraid the old man would come in drunk and start his tricks. Dave could play the piano and I was often asked to sing. I had a fair soprano voice as a boy and his family used to encourage me. They liked folk songs and I didn't go much on them, but it was a change to what I was used to. Looking back now, I am grateful to Dave and his family. Knowing them had a lot to do with my future.

Florrie was taken very queer one day; her eyes and face were swollen and she had to go to hospital. She had been painting ammunition boxes and the paint had entered a cut in her finger. She was weeks under the hospital and was not her usual self. She couldn't go to work and Mum missed her money, but she managed somehow. If she had no money there was always the pawnshop.

I remember one day I went with Mum to take a parcel to pawn. In front of us, a woman undid a blanket and put it on the counter.

'How much?' said the pawnbroker.

'Two bob,' said the woman.

The pawnbroker undid the blanket, punched it several times with his fist and said, 'Go home and take the hops out first.'

Poor woman. One laughed at the time about this, but on reflection it only shows the abject poverty that forced this woman to take a blanket off the bed. Some used the pawnshop to get money for food, some for drink. I've seen women take an ordinary flat iron, borrow 3 d. on it, get 2½ d. after ½ d. was stopped for the ticket and go straight to the nearest pub and get a half-qtn. gin. This may seem fantastic in this day and age and if anyone cares to dispute this I can name the pawnshop in Essex Road, and the pub. It took all sorts to create the poverty-stricken world we lived in.

It wasn't long before Bert and his mate came home again, six weeks at the most. As soon as they came home the old man refused to go to work. He knew they had plenty of money and he wanted to help them spend it. They were at fault in encouraging him and they would go drinking all day. I was on holiday from school and had the time of my life. Max promised to buy me a new suit. One day he took me to Gardner's Corner, Whitechapel, and I had the pick of the shop. From there he took me to a restaurant in Cable Street where he seemed to be well known.

He started to take a fancy to my sister Florrie, but she didn't go much on him. He was far too old for her, but he was very persistent. She told him time and again that she was going steady with a chap in the Navy, but he still persisted. I remember one night he asked her to go to the pictures. She told him she didn't want to go, and I remember them both looking at each other. They were fed up – Florrie wasn't well at the time, anyway. In the end she said she would go with him, but only if I could go also. Somehow he didn't seem to like this idea, but finally agreed. We walked along the Hackney Road to the Coronet Cinema. When we got there she said she had seen the film and we went home in silence. She would never be alone with him and I had to go along too on more than one occasion.

One day he had to go and sign on for a ship. I went with him to a shipping office and he signed on. Funds were getting low, so he got an advance note. This was issued by the shipping company and was an advance on wages. The note, when issued, could be cashed by the holder at a discount and made payable to the person who cashed it; as soon as the person it was issued to sailed, the value of the note could be claimed from the shipping company. Anyhow, Max went to a Jewish shop in Cable Street, got £4 for the £5 note and took me to the docks to show me his ship. I went on board with him and it was my first experience of a ship. I was astounded at the size of it and wished I was old enough to sail with him. We went back home and in the evening Max suggested they all go for a drink. About eight o'clock he said he had to see about getting away to board his ship. As it was early, someone decided we should go and see him safely aboard. Everyone went, including my young sister and myself. We all got a tram to the docks and went to find the ship. Max asked a chap where the *S. S. Weiwere* was laying. It was pitch-dark and although we had been there in daylight it was hopeless in the dark. We eventually found it and took his kit aboard. He found out it wasn't going to sail until five o'clock the following morning. Having a few bob left, he decided he had plenty of time to go back home and have a few more drinks. We found out he could get a train early next morning and he would have plenty of time to get aboard by 4am.

Needless to say, they all had one over the eight; he overslept and the ship went without him. So now he had no kit, no money and he owed the Jew £4 for defaulting on his advance note. He got out of it by signing on another ship for a longer period in order to get a bigger advance note to clear his debt. Such was the way they carried on.

This was about the time of the Battle of Jutland. Florrie was going steady with a chap on the *Queen Mary*. She had met him some three years before at Mary's wedding. His name was Charles Mason. Quite a nice chap. One Saturday afternoon his mother came round with a telegram saying he had been killed. Poor Florrie, she thought such a lot of him, and she was still very ill and not really strong enough to take the shock. For months afterwards she would visit his mother.

Gerry was getting worried. A Bill was going before Parliament for Conscription. This meant he would have to go in the army again. He could see no way out of this when his call-up came, so he started to get used to the idea. I know he got a fresh copy of his marriage certificate, making out that it had been lost, because it had been stamped when he had previously joined up.

He also started to have nights out. He told Mary he had joined a club and she somehow didn't seem to mind. On Saturday nights he said he was in a billiard game and was playing in a championship. This was supposed to run into several weeks and each week he managed to get into the next round. One Saturday night the old man invited him to a drink at the local. One drink led to another and he never went to his club.

Next morning a very nice young lady knocked on the door and asked if Gerry lived here. My sister Florrie answered the door and asked her who she was.

'I'm his young lady,' she said.

Florrie called out, 'Mary, Gerry's young lady is here.'

Gerry was out, so Mary asked her in and it seemed Gerry had been courting for months and only a week or two before had proposed to her. There was a terrific scene. When she found out Gerry was already married with a child, she asked Mary to forgive her intrusion, but she honestly didn't know. The family could understand her plight and could see she was speaking the truth. The young lady went away terribly disillusioned with all men. When Gerry came in, the fun started. Mary told him she had had a club member round to see her and when he found out what had happened he rushed out of the house, round to the local and got himself well and truly drunk. When he eventually came home, Mary and all the family were waiting on him. There was a terrible fight between him and the old man. He was an old swine, but he certainly put up a show in aid of his daughter. After the fighting had died down Mum gave him a dressing-down. He promised he would never do anything like it again and tried to apologise for all the trouble he had caused.

Mary was still crying when dinner was ready. Gerry picked up a knife to cut the joint, when suddenly he went berserk. He tried to cut his throat but the old man managed to stop him. He somehow got the knife again and managed to cut his wrists. As he drew the knife and the blood flowed, he collapsed. They rushed him to the hospital in Hackney Road. The old man warned him not to say how it happened because they would call the police if they knew it was attempted suicide, so Gerry told them he was cutting the meat and the knife slipped. He came home with his arm in a sling and everyone settled down. At night they went round to the pub, drinking up as though nothing happened. So much for Gerry's club. Although he was never trusted again, I don't think he ever went wrong again with other women.

My brother Bert and his friend Max came home again after a few weeks away and the old routine continued. The old man stayed away from work and was his usual drunken self for three to four days. I remember on this occasion their leave ran into a weekend. The Saturday morning was spent doing a round of the pubs and everyone was merry and bright, looking forward to the Saturday night. After something to eat, the old man went to sleep it off. Florrie was feeling very queer and was in bed; she was still swollen round her face and legs. After sleeping it off and having something to eat, the old man, Bert and Gerry went to the local. Mum and Mary promised to see them later. I was looking after my young sister and during the evening Mum and Mary went to have a drink with the crowd.

About nine o'clock I saw the old man stagger round the corner. I don't think I had ever seen him so bad. He evidently knew he was about to be taken short and tried to make it home. He got as far as the scullery and that was his lot. He couldn't make it. I ran upstairs to tell Florrie what had happened and we could smell him. Poor Florrie was feeling sick. He was calling out for me at the top of his voice and I didn't like to go down. Florrie told me to go and she would get up. When I went down he was still calling out but I would not go near him because of the stench.

'Stan,' he said, 'go and tell your mother I've shit myself.'

In order to get away from the smell I took to the fresh air and the local. I pushed the bar door open and tried to get Mum's eye. I eventually drew her attention and she came out with Mary.

'What's the matter?' she said.

'The old man told me to tell you he's shit himself,' I said.

'Go back and tell him to bloody well clear it up,' she said.

Back I went and there was Florrie on her hands and knees with a bowl of water clearing his mess up. Poor Florrie, she was heaving with every breath she took. Mum got back soon after me and stripped the old man and put all his clothes in the copper and made him wash in cold water. What a state to get in. This didn't stop the crowd from coming back and having their party. We never saw anything more of the old man that night.

Next day Florrie was very bad and we had to get the doctor. She must have caught a chill clearing up the night before. The doctor confined her to bed and she must have stayed there for a couple of weeks. When she was well enough to get about she couldn't go back to her old job. I think she got a light job in a sweet factory. I know I used to wait on her coming home at dinnertime. If she could she would bring me sweets, which I used to take to school.

Conscription was eventually introduced and in due course Gerry got his call-up. Worried frantic about his earlier desertion, he went for his medical and was passed A.1. He was eventually sent to Stafford and with a heavy heart he went. He swore he would get out of the army as soon as the opportunity arose.

On one of his short trips, my brother Bert brought another friend home with him and Max. His name was Bertram. He was Irish and one of the best men I have ever met. His family were in business in Dublin and he had had a wonderful education, finishing up at Dublin University. It seemed he would not toe the line at home, his father being very strict. He was a butcher and had a chain of shops in Dublin. Rather than knuckle under to his father he went to America and got various jobs. He had eventually joined the Merchant Navy, and that's how my brother came to meet him. He seemed to get on with my sister Florrie, which wasn't to the liking of Max. One wouldn't go out and leave the other at home if Florrie was there.

Bertram was also older than Florrie, but it didn't seem to matter. He didn't seem to drink like the others. They got on so well together that after a second trip they were talking about marriage. This made it awkward for Max. The fact that his friend was doing better with Florrie than he was got under his skin. In any case, Florrie would have nothing to do with him. He was told he didn't stand a chance. When their leave was up they both went to sign on their ships together – at least, that's what Max thought. To our surprise, Bertram was back on the next day. He had not signed on the same ship as Max, but had kidded him he was and had let the ship go with Max alone. His ship sailed that day and he promised that when he came back he and Florrie would get married. The trip was a long one, but he used to write us whenever he could. Max still called on his shorter trips, but knew nothing about my sister's arrangement with Bertram.

Meantime, things were very much the same with us at home. We still had the stall in Hoxton and I was still doing my trips to my uncle's. The old man wasn't doing so well now that Gerry was away and he was looking for other sources of supply. He soon made several contacts so wasn't short of money for long. Mum still managed to go down his pockets when she could, and he never knew. We were beginning to feel the effects of the food shortage now and there was yet another job for me; I had to take out my younger sister, who was now about six years old, to scrounge round the shops. We'd take a bag each and if we saw a queue forming we would line up for two pounds of potatoes. If we could not get potatoes, swedes would have to do: we had to learn to like swedes.

Owing to the air raids, Mum liked me to be within call and usually I was. I still had my friend Dave, and she thought she could be sure that if I wasn't to be found I must be with him or his parents. One time, however, things didn't work out as usual. I was in the street, early in the morning, waiting for Dave to turn up, when I saw the Cats' Meat Man. He had an enormous round in the district, selling what was known locally as 'rough', that is to say, meat for cats at a ha'penny a time and for dogs at a penny. He would deliver most days and call for the money on Saturday.

On this particular day it seemed that his helper had let him down and he asked me if I'd like to stand in and earn a few coppers. This I was always willing to do, so I quickly agreed and off we went. He had a small cart full of meat and a big basket for deliveries; he stayed by the cart, cutting up the meat in small pieces and stuck them on bits of wood, which I delivered from the basket. If people were out I shoved them through the letter boxes.

It was good fun and when dinnertime came and he took me into a coffee shop and bought me dinner, sweet and tea, I knew I was on to a good thing and didn't notice that time was getting on. We worked through the afternoon and I was thoroughly enjoying myself. Teatime arrived, and again he took me somewhere for tea and a cake. I still hadn't realised that Mum must have been wondering where I was, for it hadn't occurred to me to let her know what I was doing. We worked until quite late at night when he thanked me, gave me a shilling and told me to push off home.

I was very pleased with myself as I walked home. I had had a nice day out and was proud of what I had earned, for a shilling was hard enough to come by at the best of times. I got to the corner of our street and was surprised to see quite a crowd outside our house. As I got nearer someone shouted, 'Here he is,' grabbed me and pushed me indoors.

I'll never forget the look on Mum's face when she saw me; she was crying with relief, and when I saw that the old man was sober although it was by now well on the way to closing time I really knew that something must be up.

What was up was that I had been reported to the police as missing. Mum had got worried when I hadn't shown up by dinnertime. She made enquiries from my friends and the neighbours to no avail and by the time the old man got home she was really anxious. They decided they should tell the police and he went down to Old Street Police Station where they took particulars and told him he must bring me to the station to give an explanation if I should turn up. So down to Old Street we all went.

On arrival I was ordered to go in front of the station sergeant; the size of him scared me, but I explained what had happened as best I could. He admonished me for not telling my parents where I was. He made me promise I would never do such a thing again, and we all trooped out. We walked along the Hackney Road slowly while the old man went and got himself a pint. I never went absent again.

Gerry had now been away three months and came home on leave. He was going to France and didn't much like the idea. He still reckoned he would be out of the army as soon as the opportunity presented itself, but this time he wanted a proper discharge; no more being on the run for him.

My eldest brother Will came home from New Zealand. We were very proud of him, but somehow he seemed so distant. After being home a few days, he picked up with a girl we had all known for years and seemed to spend more time with her on his leave than with us. She caused a rift between my brother and the family and we hardly

saw anything of him during his leave. They eventually got married. None of us went to his wedding. He just was not one of us. My mother never got over his desertion of the family and in future years would not have his name mentioned.

The old man lost his job. Imports of timber were now so small that there was no need to have a salesman. They could sell what they had without him. His next job was in a warehouse in Featherstone Street, just off Old Street. He didn't earn half as much money but it was his loss rather than ours, for it simply meant he couldn't buy so much drink. The firm he worked for made furniture, brushes and all sorts of domestic woodware and he had to be packing and despatch. We wondered how long it would be before he got involved in some kind of racket. It wasn't long; he started to bring home brushes and brooms, and soon got in the money again.

We were now in 1917 and we were on the move again. Why, I cannot remember. This time we moved to Shepherdess Walk, off

City Road. It was a very large house, let off in flats. We had a ground floor and a basement flat consisting of five rooms and scullery. It wasn't a very nice place to live. We moved in the winter, which made matters worse. Food and coal were hard to come by. We all lined up for a seven-pound bag of coal; that's all we were allowed. As soon as I saw a coal-shop selling coal we would all go and line up and get our seven pounds.

During air raids, if we had time, we all used to go to the Wenlock Brewery in Wenlock Street. It had a basement and crowds used to go. It had hundreds of pipes running all round the walls and if a bomb had dropped on it we would have all drowned. It didn't take the old man long to get in where the beer was concerned.

One night he was sitting on the walls of a huge container that had thousands of gallons of beer in it and was all one mass of froth. As it was rising, his coat gradually soaked it up and he smelt like a brewery for weeks. He had a mate who worked there on night work and he often came round with a quart can of beer. He used to sit up after the pubs closed and if the warning went he was first to go down to the brewery basement and the last to leave.

My brother Bert was now on minesweepers and we hadn't seen him for months. His friend Bertram came home and we were all pleased to see him, especially Florrie. They planned to get married but times were bad.

The winter of 1917 was the worst I remember as a child. Bertram wanted to do so much for my sister. He was due back on his ship but decided to miss it. He wouldn't consider going back to sea until he got married. Obviously he had to go in hiding because the police were looking for him (not registering in those days was a crime), so we had to put him up although he had no ration card and we had to manage the best way we could. He knew his father had died and left money so he wrote to a lawyer in Dublin to see how he stood regarding his father's will. He was informed that his father had provided for him and the lawyer sent him a form to be signed by him and a Commissioner of Oaths. When sent back this would give him an advance of £50 since he was in need, and the settlement would be made at a later date. This was what he had been waiting for. He returned the completed form and to get money quickly he was prepared to borrow. Opposite was a moneylender. He went across to see him and showed him the copy of his father's will. Being an East End shyster, he saw he was on a good thing. He immediately lent him £20 at an exorbitant rate of interest, and the wedding took place. It wasn't much of a celebration. Times were too bad and everything was in short supply. The old man managed to get a bottle of whisky and a joint of meat from one of his pals in the market and they made the best of what they could get.

The problem now was for Bertram to get back to sea, but he didn't have the trouble he had anticipated. He just told the authorities he had been living in Ireland. He signed on with the Union Castle Line and was soon away.

We occasionally heard from Gerry in France and somehow he seemed well away from the fighting. He intended it to be this way if he had anything to do with it. But how long could it?

Florrie was still very queer and an appointment was made for her to see a specialist at St Bartholomew's Hospital. She was beginning to swell all over. Her legs and face were terribly swollen. As soon as the doctor saw her he admitted her straight away. It was a very bad time of the year, about three weeks before Christmas. I remember one wet and foggy Sunday we went to the hospital at the usual visiting time; she seemed fair and the Ward Sister told Mum there was a slight improvement. We were feeling jubilant to think she was getting on at last, but at eleven o'clock that night a policeman knocked on our door to tell us my sister was dangerously ill and wasn't expected to live. My mother and I got dressed and went as fast as we could to the hospital. Mum being on the big side, we couldn't hurry too much. We had to walk to City Road and get a tram to Smithfield Market. At midnight we arrived at the hospital and were shown to the ward where Florrie was. Mum and I were both tear-stained where we had been crying. The nurse showed

Mum to Florrie's bed. I wasn't allowed in and had to wait in a side ward.

With tears flowing from me, I prayed for my sister the best way I knew. I didn't know much about religion, but I felt I needed it then.

CHAPTER FIVE

We stayed at the hospital until 1am and were told they would let us know if there was any change and it was pointless to wait any longer. She was managing to hold on to life by a thread. Mum went again on Monday and it seemed that my prayers had been answered. She had passed the critical period and every hope was now given for a recovery. We were all overjoyed with the news. I was especially happy, for I loved her very much. She had always been so good to me. She was thought sufficiently recovered to be allowed to come home about a week before Christmas. She still looked very ill and was told to take things easy, which Mum saw that she did.

This was a very bad time for Mum. We no longer had the stall in Hoxton, because we couldn't buy anything to sell. The old man was still the same, drinking what he could and not caring two hoots about us. Florrie had no allowance from Bertram yet, and it was a hand-to-mouth existence. Gerry came home on leave from France; he didn't look much the worse for his experiences of the war, but he had no spare cash.

One day I had to run for the doctor. I had just come out of school and Mary was groaning in agony. The doctor came and Mary had to go to hospital immediately. The ambulance came and took her to Charing Cross Hospital and they operated on her immediately.

We were now well and truly in trouble. Florrie was still very queer and Mum had Mary's baby to look after. All this happened two days before Christmas. I knew we couldn't get anything for Christmas dinner in the shops. Mum managed to get round the old man to see one of his mates in the meat market. All he could get was a big breast of mutton and told her she was 'bleeding lucky to get that'. It wasn't a very happy Christmas.

Mary asked Mum to bring me up to see her after dinner on Christmas Day. They were having a party in the ward and tea afterwards. Mum couldn't go because of the baby and Florrie so I went with Gerry. It was a nice party. All the stars of the day showed up. One I remember in particular was Ella Shields. We all had to sing songs that were popular during the war. This was followed by a grand tea. Mary told me to eat all I could get, which I did. We arrived home about eight o'clock. Mum was nursing the baby who never seemed to stop crying. Gerry and the old man went for a drink, and stayed out until closing time, giving no thought for my mother.

We were glad to get that Christmas over. It was one of the worst in my memory.

Mary came home after two weeks and things began to settle down again.

Florrie was gradually getting better, but she found out that she was pregnant. This didn't improve her health. How, after what she had been through, she could ever manage to have a baby, nobody could see. The amazing thing was that she was improving.

We still owed the rent man. Every Monday he would knock and nearly every Monday he was told, 'We'll bring it up during the week.' Sometimes we did; most times we didn't. Consequently we were running into long arrears. I had an idea we would soon be on the move again.

We weren't alone with this thought. Next door lived a very large family. The mother and father used to go out with a horse and van and collect rags and any old junk they could get. They would unload and bring everything inside the house and all would have to work sorting the rags and breaking up the old furniture. Next morning the eldest son would take the broken furniture round to the stables and chop it up for firewood and sell it round the streets. They owed everyone. Eventually they got orders to 'Get out' and had to go. The house stood empty for some time.

Empty houses always held a fascination for us, as children, and if we could get in an empty house and play 'Mothers and Fathers' it was our delight. Usually I would play the drunken husband; I had plenty of knowledge on this sort of character. Some girl would be mother and all the smaller kids would be our children. I would come home and want to know why the dinner wasn't ready and start to clump the kids and be the tyrant father. After the game we would rummage through the house and try to imagine how and what the last tenants did. I wandered in the basement one day and saw six chairs. They looked in wonderful condition and I told Mum what I had discovered.

'Let me have a look at one,' she said. Back I went next door and got one. 'They look all right,' said Mum, 'are they all like that?'

'Yes,' I said.

She decided we would have them. I got the six chairs on the garden wall and Mum took them from me. We decided to put them under the stairs in the basement for the time being.

That night we had an air raid. We were too late to go to the Wenlock Brewery shelter, so we thought the safest place for us would be under the stairs. We set the chairs out so we could all sit down. We hadn't sat down long before one or two of us started to scratch ourselves. Soon we were all scratching. We just couldn't make out why. Suddenly Mum reckoned it was the chairs. Amid the gunfire we threw them out in the garden. They were alive with fleas. When the air raid was over we had to shake our clothes and wash.

Next day Mum sent me for a pint of paraffin and I burned them. We should have known better than to have had them in the first place. The next-door people being rag-totters we might have known they were 'alive-o'. I was not allowed in the house again.

While on the subject of air raids, I remember one Saturday morning when we had one of the worst raids of the war. Without any warning, German aeroplanes were dropping bombs all around us. The old man was home from work with the gout. On this particular occasion he was in bed with his leg up on a pillow. In those days it was a regular thing to have a 'jerry' under the bed. As the bombs were dropping, the old man went to make a quick move to get under the stairs and knocked his tobacco box into the 'jerry'. He roared and created about the 'bastard Germans'.

'All me bleeding bacca's gone,' he said.

'Serves you bloody well right,' said Mum. 'You shouldn't have the jerry under the bed, especially in the day time.'

'You don't expect me to go to the bleeding closet with a foot like this,' the old man retorted. And that's how it went on all through the raid.

My brother's friend, Max, came home again and stayed with us during the two to three days his ship was in port. He was disappointed to find my sister Florrie was married, especially to someone whom he had introduced. He spent his money like water. We always had a royal time when Max was home. It was about this time we discovered that he was a bit of a sharp boy. Just before he was due back he lost all his money gambling.

This particular day he went out about three o'clock in the afternoon and said he would be back later. About eight o'clock he came back with a Polish seaman named Silonski. He introduced him as a friend of longstanding. They brought in loads of fish and chips, bottles of beer and some rum for the old man. We couldn't understand a word this chap said. Max was the only one who could make him understand. He spoke several languages. Everyone was sitting round the table eating and drinking and the old man was well drunk and getting insulting. As he got up from the table he was rolling and he accused my mother of having an affair with Max. This was the only time I have ever been near to seeing a murder committed. Max got up and laid into the old man and nearly choked him to death. Everyone had to pull him off. The old man was going blue in the face. It was terrible. They carried him into the bedroom and he gradually came round. There was nothing a drop of rum wouldn't do for my father.

About eleven o'clock Max told Silonski it was time to go. He shook hands all round and away they went. Max was back about twelve o'clock with a roll of notes. He had evidently robbed Silonski and left him stranded. Max went away next day and we never saw him again. He must have got torpedoed and lost his life, for he would always come to see us when his ship docked.

My friend Dave from Scawfell Street kept in touch with me and still used to invite me back to his home. They were very kind people but I always felt out of place. My clothes were always so shabby in comparison with Dave's. They used to invite me chiefly to sing. I didn't mind; there was always a good spread to eat.

Florrie's time to have her baby was getting near. She was supposed to go to the Lying-In-Hospital in Old Street, but Mum wouldn't let her go owing to the air raids.

Mary had heard from the War Office that Gerry had been wounded. Afterwards the official letter said he was suffering from shell shock and was on his way home. This worried us all because we had seen some of the lads suffering from this. They used to shake from head to foot and had to be assisted in anything they did. He eventually arrived and Mary went to see him. When she came home from hospital she said his condition was fair. It was only his head that was shaking and as soon as he showed some improvement he would be allowed home for a few hours.

One Sunday afternoon, some weeks after Mary had visited him, he came home for a few hours. He had hospital-blue uniform and a stick. He had got ever so fat. We were all pleased to see him. He had a slight shake of his head. The peculiar thing was it only shook sometimes; when he was interested in anything he seemed to be quite normal. The old man noticed this and decided 'he had no bleeding shell shock – it's a put-up job to get out of the bloody army'. He waited for him to leave before he said this, but I must admit the old man seemed right.

Florrie had her baby. It was a little girl. A sweet little thing and we called her Flossie.

We now needed more room, so it was on the move again when Florrie was well enough. Mum, Mary and Florrie wanted a house where we could all live together with plenty of room. They saw one in Bridport Place – No. 41. It was a large flat-fronted house with two storeys above ground floor. How they ever managed to get such a place I don't know. The landlords must have been glad to let houses to anyone. If references had been required we could never produce one. We were now back to where my story first started. We had to get a horse and van to move with. Mary had the ground floor, Florrie the first floor, we had the top floor and the old man had his favourite pub, the Bridport Arms. I knew the area well and we knew most of the people around.

Gerry got his ticket from the army with a pension. I don't think it was much. He got his job back in Bethnal Green, and he and the old man were considering going back again into the glue and screw racket. I would not have anything to do with it this time and told my mother I didn't want to. She told them in no uncertain terms where to get off and Gerry had to manage with what he could bring home at nights.

I did get involved in a glue racket my father started on his own, but I was unsuspecting.

He asked me one day to meet him at dinnertime with a barrow; this was on a Saturday. As soon as my mother knew, she refused to let me go.

'It's nothing pinched,' he said. 'It's only a sack of firewood I want him to take to someone.'

Believing him she let me go. I took the barrow to Featherstone Street, Old Street, and the firm was shut. I waited outside a few minutes and the gate shutters were pulled up enough for me to go in. The old man and another chap humped a huge sack on the barrow and told me to take it to Brick Lane where he would meet me. I stopped under the arch at Great Eastern Street for a rest. I looked at the sack and thought I had never seen firewood in such accurate shapes. I undid the string stitching at the corner of the sack and saw it was cakes of Scotch glue. I knew I had been taken in.

When the old man arrived I told him what I had discovered and I intended to tell my mother when I got home. I was getting old enough now to talk to him. He knew I had not wanted to help him pinch things; I was seeing too many of my schoolmates being put away for thieving for me to want to do anything like that. He begged me not to split on him.

'Don't tell your mother and I'll give you half a crown,' he said.

Never having had half a crown, I accepted. When he unloaded the glue he gave me two and six, and made me promise not to tell.

'I might want you to come again next week,' he said, and the half-crown came to my mind. I said I would go. When I got home I told Mum I got two and six from the man I took the firewood to. I gave her one and six and went to the pictures that night.

Opposite the house was a small general shop. They sold groceries and at the back was a large shed. The chap who owned the shop was a cabinetmaker and he worked in the shed while his wife ran the shop. I often used to go and watch him at work. He told me he just could not get glue and asked me if I knew where any could be got.

'If you get any, Stan, I would give you two and six a pound for it.' They were his words and I began to think. I found myself a small sack and looked forward to next Saturday.

The following Friday night the old man asked me to come to the usual place with a barrow. I told him I would get the sack unloaded at the shop where he took it last week as I was in a hurry to get back. He said that would be O. K. and he would see me when he got back. I got the barrow loaded and was on my way. I had a stop at the usual place, under the railway arch at Great Eastern Street, and started to undo the stitching on the sack. I took out eight cakes of glue and put them in my own bag. I then delivered the glue and was off home. Before going home I took my bag into the grocer's shop and told the lady I had managed to get her husband his glue. She called him out and he was delighted. He weighed it and gave me ten shillings. I went home and told my mother what I had done. She was annoyed to think I had gone against her wishes. I gave her seven and sixpence and told her there was no risk. In any case, it was the old man's responsibility. I was only doing as I was told.

I had never had the fantastic sum of five shillings in my pocket. I was very sweet on a girl who lived opposite. Her name was Mary and we used to meet when we came out of school and walked home together. She invited me to her home on one or two occasions. Her father was crippled, as a result of the war, and her mother used to make handmade cigarettes at home. It was through her I learned to smoke. Mary would often give me a few cigarettes and I would smoke them on the quiet.

Anyhow, with five shillings in my pocket I thought I would give Mary a night out. I asked her mother if I could take her to the Olympia in Shoreditch. She gave me permission and we had two seats in the pit. This, plus sweets and fruit, soon made a hole in my five shillings. I didn't mind though; she was a nice girl and worth it. We saw a revue called *The Byng Boys are Here*. We did this outing on two or three occasions when I could get the money.

To help out at home, I got myself a job after school hours at a small printers. I was learning to work a Platen printing machine. I got four and six a week, and had to work from five o'clock till eight o'clock and Saturday mornings. The August holidays came around and I was offered a full month's work. Ten shillings a week, eight o'clock to six o'clock. I readily agreed and started on Monday morning of the first week of the holidays. Being opposite the house, I was told I could go home for morning tea. I went home at ten-thirty and was just drinking my tea when Bertram, my sister Florrie's husband, walked in from sea.

We hadn't heard from him in months. He went crazy when he saw his baby. She was lovely and he was like a little boy with a new toy. He undid his kitbag and he brought out sugar, tea, tins of milk, ham and all foodstuffs we couldn't buy. I was proud to tell him I was working during my school holidays. He told me I shouldn't do it as I would have enough work when I left school. When I told him we needed the money he told me not to worry, he would see to that. He had to go back to the docks to get paid off and asked me to go with him. I went to tell the printer I wouldn't be back any more and he wasn't too pleased; he had lost a good bargain. Sixty hours work for ten shillings. I wasn't worried about him though; I was looking forward to going with my brother-in-law.

After dinner we went and he took me over to the ship. It was a Union Castle ship called the *Galway Castle*. I was amazed at the size of it. I began to wish I was old enough to sign on. After about an hour he had to go to the office to get paid off. He came out with a stack of pound-notes. I had never seen so much money. We went into a restaurant and he told me to have just what I wanted. He gave me a royal time. When we got home he gave my sister most of his money and gave me the £2 which I would have earned if I had gone to work. I gave most of this to Mum, who promised she would put it towards a new suit she had promised me. It was a long time since I had had a suit, and was looking forward to it. I got it eventually and Mum promised it wouldn't go to pawn. I was so used to wearing 'hand me downs' that I couldn't believe it.

Bertram told us he would only be home until the Thursday. As he only had three more days leave, he intended to live it up. At night he asked Gerry (who had somehow made a marvellous recovery), the old man and all who cared to go for a 'booze-up' at the Bridport. It must have seemed like old times at the Bridport Arms for the old man and the family to be back. They all had a right royal time and brought back plenty of drink. This was usual at the time. Anyone who came home on leave always had a beer-up. We still had a gramophone and they nearly danced the floor in.

Gerry and the old man were soon at it again. They just could not agree when they had been drinking. There was the usual fight between the two of them and Gerry got the shakes. He went berserk, opened the window and was going to jump out. My sisters screamed and managed to hold him back after much struggling. I was standing outside and saw the window go up amid a lot of shouting and screaming, but I have often wondered since if he would really have jumped. When the old man saw him open the window and attempt to jump he is supposed to have said, 'Let him bleeding well jump

78

and good riddance'. They got Gerry to bed and had to send for a doctor. All the doctor told him was to lay off the drink as it was aggravating his complaint.

There was no work for anyone next morning. When Gerry and the old man met they just glared at each other. Peace was made by an invitation by Bertram for 'a quiet one at the Bridport'. By one o'clock they were all good pals again.

Bertram's three days soon went and amid many tears he went back. Mum thought the world of him and she was heartbroken to see him go.

Mum was getting sick of the old man and Gerry fighting and rowing every weekend when they had been drinking and suggested to Mary that they should find a place of their own. It wasn't much of a life for anyone and she agreed to move if she could. My girl-friend who lived opposite happened to mention to me one day that a flat was empty in the house where she lived. I told Mary and she went across to have a look at it. She decided to take it and I was pleased because this gave me an opportunity to see more of my girl.

About September 1918, Mary moved and we were now left with a house that was too big for us, so Mum and Florrie started to look around for another place. They found a six-roomed flat over a dairy in New North Road, and we moved again. I have never heard of a family that moved more than we did; perhaps we must have had a gipsy trait in us somewhere.

We now lived in a very nice place on the main road. The rooms were large and there was always something going on. Florrie had two rooms, we had the other four. The old man was still working at the same place and still keeping my mother short of money. She was now taking in dressmaking. This meant she was on the machine from morning till night. The old man still came home every night and weekends the worse for drink. It still wasn't very pleasant, but the war was getting towards the end and we were hoping for better things.

One Saturday afternoon, we were all having tea when a telegram arrived for Florrie. It was from the Union Castle Shipping Line, telling her that the *Galway Castle* had been torpedoed and there were fears for the safety of her husband. We couldn't believe we would never see Bertram again. We tried all ways to kid Florrie that he must have been saved, but she wouldn't have it. We got an evening paper and it was all over the front page. The paper said only a few survivors. We tried to tell Florrie that he might be among them. During the week, we had confirmation that he had been missing and was now presumed dead. We managed to get the address of one of the survivors and my father and I went to see him in order to comfort my sister. The chap knew Bertram and said he was on watch at the time the ship was torpedoed and didn't stand a chance. So my sister, a bride of a few months, was left a widow with little Flossie. She was given a pension and £300 was granted by the shipping company as compensation. This had to be drawn when she was in need, at the discretion of the Court.

Armistice was declared on November 11th and the worst war in history was over. People were going mad with joy. The streets were packed with men and women singing and dancing and the pubs sold out of beer, much to my father's disgust. While all this celebration was going on, poor Florrie was sitting at the window, with little Flossie on her lap, crying. We couldn't do much with her. Mum told me to go round to Mary and see if she and Gerry would come around. When Mary saw the state Florrie was in she suggested we all go out. Gerry reckoned it would be a good plan to go to Homerton and see his mother and father. It would get Florrie out, so we all got ready and took the bus to Homerton. The old man wouldn't come. He was in pursuit of any pub that had beer. Gerry's mum was glad to see us all. She got something to eat and Gerry and his father got some drink from somewhere and they celebrated the end of the war in their own way. Gerry found a shop that was selling fireworks and he bought me some. Half of them were duds. They had been in stock since 1913. As the time went on, Florrie gradually got used to the idea of never seeing Bertram again, and settled down.

The war had robbed the district of many familiar people, but one of those who came back was 'Uncle George', who was the husband of one of my mother's friends, Annie South. Uncle George was a rag-and-bone man and they had a pretty drab existence.

Many is the time on a Monday morning when he would knock on our door and ask Mum if she could 'lend him a start'. This meant that he wanted to borrow a shilling as capital for his day's trading. If she had one to lend, he always got it and always paid her back as soon as he had bought and sold enough rags. He was in the Reserves and I remember him coming to kiss us goodbye in 1914. A few months later he came back minus a leg. Somehow he did not seem to mind; at least, he and his family would never starve again. His pension would see to that.

This was my last year at school and I was very big for my age. I tried to get myself a job after school hours, and eventually found one. I was passing a big old house when I happened to see a board outside with the name and stating they were artificial-flower manufacturers. I knocked and went in and asked if they wanted a boy to make himself useful after school. When the governor saw how big I was he offered me a job cutting out leaves for the flowers at four shillings a week. I accepted and soon learned the ropes. I had to stand at a bench which had a huge square of lead 18 inches by 18 inches by 4 inches. Some green shiny material was folded into six thicknesses. A steel stamp cut out the leaves when I whacked it with a seven-pound hammer. I did this from five o'clock until eight o'clock each evening and I knew I had been working. I stuck it out, though, and the few bob came in handy at home.

My brother Bert came home from the Far East. He had been mine-sweeping. He didn't stay home long. He found himself a girl-friend and went to stay with her people. This was all right while the money lasted, but when he was broke, back he came. He couldn't

81

settle down. He just had to have discipline. He tried many jobs but couldn't keep one longer than a week.

Mum had a lot to put up with. Things should have been better for her now we were nearly all grown up, but it didn't work out that way for her. There was always a problem of some sort that held her back. Bert was ill for a long time. He had caught some sort of tropical disease out East and was attending hospital.

Now yet another problem was in store for Mum. One Sunday afternoon Florrie took her baby to see some friends. She was in black at the time and it didn't take passers-by long to see she was a widow. On the way home, as she was waiting for the bus at Old Street Station, a chap came up and asked her if he could help her with the baby. He was in the Royal Navy Air Service and looked very smart. He saw my sister home and she asked my mother if she could bring him in. Mum told her she was her own mistress and could do as she liked. She brought him in and they seemed to take to one another straight away. His name was Arthur and he was expecting his demob very soon. He called again next day, and did so regularly for a week or two.

He had been married before but was now divorced. They decided to settle down and get married as soon as he was demobbed. This started the family talking. One reckoned she should be ashamed of herself so soon after Bertram's death. Mum wouldn't get involved. She told her she hoped she knew what she was doing; what did she know about him? Nothing. What had caused the divorce and who was to blame? All these things came up but it was no use. Florrie had made up her mind. Mum tried to tell her to wait a bit longer but it was no use. The old man made it plain that he didn't like Arthur, but nobody took any notice of him – he didn't like anybody.

When Arthur got demobbed they got married and came to live with us. We thought we had the Duke of Wapping living with us. He did fancy his weight. He dressed in Harris-tweed suits, walking stick, felt velour hat; he had the lot.

'Who the bleeding hell does he think he is?' the old man would say.

He would ignore me and my young sister Amelia. He'd pass us on the stairs without a remark. Gerry couldn't stand him. Mary wouldn't speak to him. She said she felt awkward when he spoke to her. Nobody in the family could get on with him. If anyone complained to my mother about him ignoring us she would tell us to take no notice. Any complaint to Florrie fell on deaf ears. She wouldn't have a word said against him. He was just self-centred and thought we were all beneath him.

He used to take Florrie to the West End and we would have little Flossie to look after until they came home. We began to notice that Florrie was always short of money. She started to go to the Court to get a grant from the £300 the shipping company had put in trust for her. Arthur was back at his old job on the Railway as a ticket collector. He still ignored us; he would come home and hardly show his face. He never spoke of the past and no mention was ever made of his former wife.

One day we had another shock. Mr Marshall, who owned the dairy downstairs, came up and asked to see the old man. He and Gerry were discussing who was going to win the Derby. Gerry thought Panther would win and the old man couldn't see anything to beat Lord Glanelly's Grand Parade. This was the first post-war Derby and whenever these two met arguments and discussions on the merits of horses always seemed to be the topic of the day. I broke up the discussion by telling the old man Mr Marshall wanted to see him. He told me to ask him in. He shocked us by saying he was going to sell the dairy and we would have to quit the flat. He told us he had a house at Walthamstow we could rent and he would pay all expenses if we would move.

In 1919 Walthamstow to us was like moving to the country. The whole family discussed the matter and it was agreed they would go and see the place. The old man was against going. Florrie didn't like the idea because of the distance from Arthur's work. After seeing the house nobody thought much of it and conveyed their feelings to Mr Marshall. He explained that he had offered us alternative accommodation. If we didn't go he would have no choice but to take us to Court to get us out.

Places to live in were now getting harder to find, so under the circumstances it looked as though we were on our way.

CHAPTER SIX

We moved to Walthamstow in the first week of July 1919. It was a small house just off the High Street. The rent was eight shillings per week. Florrie and Arthur came with us and had to manage in one room. There were five of us and we needed the rest of the house. Arthur had to get a transfer to Manor House Station. This journey he did by cycle every day. The old man had to go to Liverpool Street every day and swore and cursed about the journey. He used to catch the six-thirty workman's train each morning. The fare was twopence return. I had three weeks to go before I was fourteen, and thought I could start work without going to another school. This I was not allowed to do, and had to finish my time at Pretoria Avenue School. I was mad about this but try as I might I had to go until my birthday came. I was anxious to start work. I tried working in a grocer's shop, but didn't like it. I wanted to do something more constructive, and where I could get the most money.

The old man said he would put a word in for me at his place, and one night he came home and told me he had spoken to the Mill foreman and I was to go next morning for an interview at ten o'clock. I got up early and caught the six-thirty with my old man. I went with him to a coffee shop and had something to eat. He started at eight o'clock, so I had two hours to waste. I walked about some of my old haunts in Hoxton and was outside the office at ten prompt. I was told to start next day. My wage was to be £1 a week. I didn't expect so much money and was delighted to think I would be able to help out at home. I told Mum the good news and it was arranged I should have six shillings and Mum fourteen. This seemed a fair arrangement to me.

I started work next morning and from there I learned my trade as a woodworking machinist and cabinetmaker. It was all very strange at first. The noise on entering the sawmills was deafening and I didn't think I would stick the day out, but I soon got used to it.

Things were now better at home for my mother. My bit of money was regular and with the bit of dressmaking she was doing she managed to get by.

I was beginning to like our new surroundings. For a penny you could get into Epping Forest, and this was all so different to the slums of Hoxton and Bethnal Green. My friend Dave would come some weekends and we had some good times together in the forest.

With Florrie, however, things were plainly not going at all well, and Mum took her aside and asked her what the trouble was. Mum could see that she had started to pawn things and that her compensation money had run out. She said she just could not manage on Arthur's money. She said she couldn't ask him to give her more, but Mum made her have a showdown. He soon knuckled down, but now he was more in his shell than ever. He still continued to ignore everybody. Florrie was now beginning to see where she had gone wrong. They had a terrible row and in the end she told him to go. He went out and then he came back for his things. She packed his case, threw it out of an upper window and away he went. About two hours later he crept back and they had a reconciliation, on her terms. Looking back now, I suppose there wasn't much else she could do with the baby coming. He toed the line afterwards and Florrie's word was law. He never attempted to hold back money from her again and, in the end, we all got to know each other better.

The old man was still getting his drink. I used to come back on the same train as him on leaving work, but he would always get out at St James Street Station and go straight to his local, the Cock Tavern in the High Street. Soon he got into the habit of taking days off. The ranks of the unemployed were swelling and Mum used to tell him that one day he would get the sack. True enough he did. He came home one Friday night and said he had got put off. This wasn't going to make any difference to my mother regarding money, so she didn't worry too much. He used to go out at eleven o'clock in the morning, come home at three o'clock, sleep during the afternoon and go out again at six o'clock until ten o'clock. All the money he got from the Labour Exchange he kept and spent on beer.

To raise an extra few shillings, he took on the job of runner to a local bookmaker. He would stand outside the Cock and between pints would collect bets. He and his pals had taken a brick out of the wall in the Gent's lavatory at the side of the pub and every half-hour the old man would go out to the lavatory, take out the loose brick, put the bets in the recess and replace the brick. The book-maker would call at regular intervals, collect the bets and be away. The cash was paid in when the pub closed. This was done in case the old man got picked up by the police. He was questioned several times but nothing was ever found on him to prove he had been taking bets. One day, though, he did get done.

He was paying out two women and there was an argument about threepence. He wouldn't have it that they were right and, to prove his point, started to reckon the bet up. During the argument, un-beknown to him, a plain-clothes policeman had been listening and watching, for he had been suspected for some time. As he showed the old ladies his piece of paper with the bet reckoned up, the policeman came and grabbed him. He had to appear at Stratford and got fined £5. He had no time for old women after that.

About December 1920 I had a bad bout of bronchitis. My mother took me to St Bartholomew's Hospital and after examination I was told to give up my job in the sawmills as the wood dust would ruin me. This was a blow as I was the only one at work in my family, but my mother insisted that I must give the job up. I tried hard to get an outdoor job, but there were about two million unemployed and it was impossible to get any sort of job. I wasn't old enough for sick-ness or unemployment benefit and things were pretty grim. The old man had run out of his unemployment benefit and was on public relief. The Relieving Office gave him eight shillings in money for the rent and the rest in food tickets which hardly enabled us to exist.

Mum was trying to get me new-laid eggs for my chest, which she used to heat up in milk. I know she used to go without herself to give me eggs and milk. My brother Bert was only getting fifteen shillings on the Labour Exchange. The old man used to keep the eight shillings and give Mum the food tickets. I was earning nothing. Nearly everyone we knew was in similar circumstances.

About three weeks before Christmas 1921 Mum had a letter from Mary saying Gerry was out of work and they were having a rough time. Could they come and stay with us for Christmas? Mum and Florrie talked it over and asked them to come about ten days beforehand. I had to give up my bed, so did my brother, and at night we made a bed up on the floor. Mum was determined to give us all a good Christmas. Weeks before, she made up frocks and trousers out of anything she could lay her hands on. A week before Christmas she found a space for a small barrow in the High Street market and sold most of the things she had made up.

Meanwhile, Gerry hadn't been idle. He had seen an advertisement for cheap Christmas cards and reckoned if he could borrow the money to buy a couple of hundred he would do all right. He asked Mum and, always a soft touch, she lent him £1, which was a fortune to her, telling him if he lost it in the venture there would be no Christmas dinner. He bought the cards, went and got some old wooden boxes, made himself a stall and stood in the High Street. I must hand it to Gerry that he wasn't lazy. Someone lent him a tarpaulin to make a cover and he was well set.

The first three days he sold out. He'd made a fair profit and took a chance and bought four hundred cards. He only had four days in which to sell them. One of these four days disaster nearly caught him. The wind was blowing a gale and Mary asked me to take him a jug of tea and some sandwiches. Just as I got there a gust of wind blew his stall up in the air and landed in the middle of the road. Poor Gerry, the look of despair on his face as the Christmas cards were blowing all up the High Street. We managed to salvage most of them. Luckily it wasn't raining. In the end he succeeded in selling all his cards at a good profit; he paid Mum back and was well set for a good Christmas.

By night-time on Christmas Eve, everyone was set for a good session at the Cock Tavern in the High Street. There was Gerry, the old man and my brother Bert. Mum, Florrie and Mary and the children were at home getting everything ready for Christmas. About ten-thirty the trio came home, loaded with drink inside and out. They had a gallon jar each and several bottles.

According to Bert they had been in a fight. Evidently someone was taking it out on the old man, an argument developed and a fight started. By all accounts they must have got the advantage as they were all merry and bright. Arthur was on late turn on the Railway and when he got in they welcomed him with a drink. To everyone's amazement, he took it. As they were all drinking up and singing, there was a loud knock on the door. I opened up and a huge chap was standing there with a notebook. He asked for the old man by name. I went and told him he was wanted.

'Who the hell wants me on Christmas Eve?' he said.

'Go and see,' I told him.

He went to the door and this chap told him he was a detective-inspector, looking into the fight that had taken place previously. Everyone went out in the street and a right argument took place.

As they were arguing, a small stocky chap and his wife were passing the door and heard the argument. He stopped and listened and heard the so-called detective ask them all to accompany him to the station.

'Ask him for his warrant,' said the stranger.

'Yes,' said Gerry, 'I never thought of that – where *is* your warrant?'

The detective stood under the street lamp and started trying to find the warrant, which he never had. By this time the stranger felt really involved.

'You're no bleeding tec,' he said and with that he gave him a real right-hander straight to the chin. Down went the detective, knocked out cold.

'Good night all,' said the stranger, and away he went, leaving his wife behind. She told us he was a boxer and a real terror. From round the corner four or five people came running and saw the 'detective' lying in the road. They explained to Florrie that he wasn't a real detective but just a friend of one of the people who had got the worst of the fight trying to frighten Gerry and the old man into believing he was.

In the end, the tec recovered, everyone went inside and made it up, apologised and departed the best of friends; all promised to see each other at the Cock on Christmas morning. And they did. That was typical of Gerry and the old man. If they weren't fighting each other, they'd fight someone else.

The following evening all got together for a real beer-up. Where the old man had found the money, I just don't know. During the evening everyone wanted to know where Arthur was. Florrie said he wouldn't come down. He had a row with the old man previously and would only come down if the old man apologised; he was like that. He thought there was only one person right in the world and that was him. In order to keep the peace and get the party going, the old man went up and apologised to Arthur. It was one of the few occasions I ever felt sorry for him, as I knew what it must have meant for his pride. Arthur came down in the end and everyone got going.

Christmas ended, and, to everyone's surprise, no more fights. The day after Boxing Day, Mary and Gerry went home and we got back to normal.

Nothing much happened during the first two or three months of 1922. My health improved and I was feeling much better, but I still could not get employment of any kind.

About March things became desperate at home. We were living below subsistence level but the old man was still somehow managing to get enough money to buy drink with. Mum became suspicious that perhaps he was using the rent money. He was supposed to pay the rent every Friday afternoon when he got the money from the

Relieving Office. She hadn't seen the rent book for weeks and when she approached him about it he would say they kept the book at the rent office. One day Mum asked me to look around the bedroom to see if he had hidden it anywhere. I looked in every conceivable place but couldn't find it anywhere. I was on the point of giving up when suddenly I noticed a crack in the corner of the lino. I lifted it up and there was the rent book. When we checked up, he hadn't paid for eight weeks.

When he came home after three o'clock there was one almighty row. How could he have done such a thing? My poor mother had to rake around and get a few things together to try and make a parcel to pawn in order to get a couple of weeks' rent so that we could save ourselves from getting notice to quit. Mum and Florrie managed to raise enough for two or three weeks' rent between them and Florrie took it to the rent office and explained what my father had done. They told her we would have got notice to quit long beforehand but that they had felt so sorry for him that they had put it off. He was never trusted to pay the rent after that.

By now I was about sixteen and a half, and I decided that it would be best for all if I were to try to join the army, so I went to Whitehall and asked to join the Royal Garrison Artillery. I had a medical but was told to come back after a rest. I went and sat outside for an hour and went back again. After another examination I was duly accepted, given a day's pay and told to call every day until my references had come through.

When I got home and told Mum what I had done she burst into tears and asked me why I had to do such a thing. I gave her my reason but she didn't see my point of view. I went to Whitehall every day for three days and each morning my mother used to see me off at the door crying. I was duly accepted and went to Woolwich for training. This wasn't so bad, as I managed to get home most weekends. I got eighteen shillings per week and made an order to Mum for five shillings a week. This was a great help to her. She still had my young sister Amelia at home but somehow she got by.

After being stationed at Woolwich for three months I was sent for gunnery training at Southsea. After passing out, I was put on draft to Malta and given a month's leave. During this leave I could see things getting worse at home. The old man's dole had been stopped and he had to work on public relief work to earn his relief. This didn't amount to much and by the time he had his share Mum was left with almost nothing.

Much as I liked being in the army, I knew that, as I was still under seventeen, I could get out on compassionate grounds if I could find someone prepared to employ me. I tackled the milkman who had a one-man business and asked him if he would give me a job if I got out of the army. After a lot of discussion he promised me a job at thirty-five shillings a week. I told Mum what I intended to do and she was delighted. I told her and Florrie that when my leave was finished and I returned to Southsea they were to write to my Commanding Officer, explaining I was barely seventeen and asking them to discharge me on the grounds of my age and the fact that I was wanted to help keep our home together by taking the job I was offered.

A week after my return to barracks, I was called into the Company Office and told by my Commanding Officer that they had received a letter from my mother. After asking me about conditions at home, he was very sympathetic and told me I would be recommended for discharge, but I would have to wait a little. Meanwhile I was to be taken off the Malta draft and given a job as storekeeper.

One morning I received a letter from my sister Florrie telling me little Flossie had passed away. I was stricken with grief and couldn't believe it. She had grown into a beautiful child and it just didn't seem possible. I showed the letter to my sergeant, who immediately granted me ten days leave. I got home as soon as I could and the house was like a morgue. Even the old man was upset. It seemed that little Flossie had got diphtheria and this was only discovered when it was too late to save her.

We got as much money together as we could and started to make arrangements for the funeral. Gerry and Mary were staying with us at the time. They bought what black they could afford and Mary suggested dyeing several articles black, so she and Florrie got a bath of water and started dyeing. When they were nearly through it was discovered the old man never had any black trousers, so I gave him a pair of khaki slacks, which Mary and Florrie promptly started to dye black. As they had already used up most of the power of the dye, the trousers became only dark green. To make them black Mary suggested putting soot in the water, which she did. They had to let it go at that and they were duly dried and pressed.

It was a sad day when we buried little Flossie; we just could not believe we would never have her with us again. After the service, we were coming home in the coach when a watery sun started to shine through the window. It settled on the old man's trousers. Sad as the occasion was, we somehow had to laugh. The sun brought out the colour in his trousers and black and green patches appeared. As soon as Mary saw them she winked at Florrie and pointed to the trousers. Remembering the caper they had cut when they were doing the dyeing, they both found it hard to keep back their giggles.

I will say this for my family; however sad the occasion there was always someone who would try to raise a laugh.

I duly returned from leave and was given my discharge in December 1922. Mum and Florrie were glad I was home and hoped I would settle down. My first move was to the milkman who promised me a job. He was sorry, he said, but things were bad and he couldn't see his way clear to employ me.

So now I was back where I started. I just did not know where to turn for a job. Christmas was a week or so away and it looked like being another grim one. As usual, Mum had made up a load of frocks and coats and sold them in the High Street which got us our Christmas.

After Christmas things were worse than ever. If I could get twopence I would walk to Shoreditch and Bethnal Green, and try all the cabinet-making dives in the East End. After doing the rounds, I would get a tram back to Walthamstow for twopence, but it seemed hopeless and I would have done better to stay at home and save my boot-leather.

From 1922 till 1925 I got odd jobs anywhere I could, but most of the time I was out of work. If I had enough stamps on my card I would get fifteen shillings per week unemployment benefit. If I hadn't, I got nothing.

CHAPTER SEVEN

If we had a shilling, a friend and I would go to a dance. Sometimes I would ask Florrie to lend me Arthur's shoes or his jacket and vest. It was at one of these dances, in 1924, that I met my wife. We grew very much in love. She had lost her mother and was keeping house for her father and three brothers and was doing a colossal job. I was introduced to her family and duly accepted. They were a wonderful family and in over forty years I have never had a bad word with any one of them; one brother in particular became a close friend and remains so now after all these years.

But I was still out of work and had nothing; not a very good prospect for one who was courting a girl! I used to get home at night and lie awake for hours wondering what the future could hold for me.

One night I had a brainwave. I wrote a letter to the manager of the Labour Exchange telling him my father was going to throw me out as he just could not afford to keep me any longer. Two days after, I signed the register for work and was called into the Manager's Office. He told me how sorry he was to think things had come to such a pass at home and that he would make a special effort to try and find me a job.

About a week after, I was called in to see the Manager again. He told me a job was going in Holloway Road making ebony goods, but did I know how to work an oscillated spindle? I said firmly yes that I had had previous experience. He gave me a pretty doubtful look which was fully justified as I had never heard of an oscillated spindle and hadn't a clue as to what it was. However, I stood my ground and was told to go along and was given a green card. I had no money for the fare, so went home and borrowed Arthur's bike. I had the interview for the job and got it. I was told to start next morning and asked how much money I wanted. When I said one and threepence an hour, the Manager nearly fell on his face. After much haggling we settled for one shilling. I was bucked to death to think I had a start at last. I got no sleep that night wondering how I would get on next day. I had to beg and borrow for my fare to Holloway Road. I duly started work and prayed I would master the machine, which I eventually did. I am sure the chaps felt sorry for me and gave me a great deal of help. I didn't get the sack that night, so went home tired but happy.

On the Friday night I went to the Labour Exchange to tell them I got the job. The Manager was flabbergasted. He told me the job had been going for three months and they could not find anyone with experience. It just goes to show.

I was now able to help out at home and soon got on my feet. My flat rate was £2 7s. 6d. a week and from August to December there was plenty of overtime. By Christmas I had managed to save enough to rig myself out and to get engaged. After Christmas 1925, Lilian and I decided we would like to get married. She was having a tough time of it being housekeeper to four men, and things were not very good at my home. We struggled to save every shilling we could get.

By March 1926 my father's legs began to swell. He was advised to give up drinking, but refused. Mum was worried about him, but there was nothing any of us could do. His whole life had been given to drink and it was too late now.

Lilian and I went ahead with our plans to get married and decided to do so on July 31st, but we could not get a place to live in for love or money. In the last couple of weeks, when we were getting desperate, a friend at work told me his mother had a nice room for rent. Lilian and I went along, saw it and decided to have it on the spot. Our landlady was a delightful person and gave us every help.

Meantime, my father had become bedridden. His whole body had swollen to a terrific size, and he seemed to be just waiting to die, but he still had his old drinking pals who came to see him and they would bring him in bottles of beer.

Lilian and I got married and Lilian's people gave us a nice reception. Obviously, the old man couldn't come, and neither could my mother as she had to stay with him, but she gave us her blessing which she meant from the bottom of her heart. We soon settled in our new home and were very happy.

Within three months my father died. Mum told us that two nights before, he had got one of his pals to sell his trousers and get beer with the money. My mother was left with the princely sum of two farthings, his remaining wealth.

At this point in my life, I end the present narrative, though I hope to continue in a further book of reminiscences, if this book is well received by the public. Mum died in 1946; my sister Florrie in 1947 and my brothers Will in 1954 and Bert in 1950. Only my two other sisters, Mary and Amelia, and myself have survived. Gerry died in 1960, leaving Mary with three fine sons who are rarely out of her company. Amelia has one son who is a director of research at one of our greatest Universities. I am still blessed with the love of my wife and that of three good sons who are all making their way in the world. Florrie left one son and two daughters, whom we see frequently and are most kind and considerate to my wife and myself.

So, out of so disastrous a childhood, I am now surrounded, in spite of poor health, with love and happiness – a happiness always denied to my poor mother without whom we should all have either starved or become criminals. Looking back, I still keep asking myself how *she* survived and why she chose to stay with a man like my father. In recent years I have become a believer in the afterlife and, if my beliefs are correct, she has found her happiness there. Once through a well-known London medium, my mother told me, speaking of my father, that he was 'more sinned against than he sinned'; this I have never understood, but perhaps she saw qualities in him or had some knowledge of him that was not evident to us, and this accounted for her loyalty.

POSTSCRIPT

These memoirs first appeared in *Profile*, the magazine of the Hackney Borough Library Services, which enjoys a large circulation in the district where the events it describes took place. Both the library authorities and I were surprised and delighted by the interest it aroused. Many letters were received, not only from the borough itself but from former residents overseas.

These letters told of similar memories and similar experiences, so I am satisfied that the picture I have tried to draw was neither exceptional nor one-sided.

Talking to middle class people who did not live in working class districts, I find that few realise how bad conditions were such a comparatively short time ago. ('Your story reads more like something out of Dickens,' was a typical comment.) It was easy, it seems, for the better-off to be unaware of the appalling poverty and near starvation that existed.

But those of us (and there are plenty) who remember lining up in the snow at the local Mission for a jug of soup or second-hand boots, begging for relief at the Poor Law Institution, being told to take our caps off and address officials as 'Sir,' realise it all too well. Yet amid those terrible times, we found time to laugh. We did not expect many pleasures out of life, but those we could get we took to the full. Perhaps it was this that enabled *us* to survive and perhaps this is why some of my older readers said they looked back with nostalgia and even affection to some aspects of those old days.

To my younger readers, may I say, 'Be thankful that you were born now and not then. Go forward, but try to be tolerant of your parents on the way.'

THE
YEARS
AFTER

Illustrated by
JOE McLAREN

FOREWORD

When I wrote part one of *A Hoxton Childhood* I never intended to go any further. It was only intended to be a comparison of life as it was in the early part of the century to be given to my sons, grandchildren, nieces and nephews as a record of my early life.

People have often asked me, 'Surely with such a childhood, there must be lots of happenings that you could write about in your grown-up life?'

I have decided to accept this challenge after much thought, but I have only mentioned the highlights of 40 years' happenings. I sincerely hope part two, *The Years After*, proves as interesting to the reader as part one.

A. S. JASPER

CHAPTER ONE

I must go back to 1926. Lilian and I were engaged and very much in love. As I have explained previously, she had not had much of a life for a 20-year old girl. Her mother died when she was 15, and Lilian was left to keep house for her father and three brothers. However, Lilian reckoned she could still keep house for them after we were married, just like any other woman who went to work.

I had to agree to this arrangement, otherwise we were likely to be apart for years to come. We decided on the date, which was to be the 31st of July 1926. We had managed to get one room in Tottenham, so we were all set. I was only earning £2 7s 6d at the time, but we saved every penny we could and managed to buy all the small items we needed. The biggest items were the furniture. We didn't need all that much for one room, but the total cost was in the region of £50. We finally decided to get the furniture on hire purchase. I think we paid £5 down and the balance was supposed to be paid at 6/- per week. A week before our wedding, the furniture arrived. What a thrill we got setting it all out! It looked lovely, and the great day could not come soon enough for us. In those days there was no such thing as paid holidays. Like it or leave it, my firm shut down for ten days, and we had to manage as best we could.

So, my first two weeks of married life started without a penny coming in from anywhere. This didn't daunt us, and we knew we would get over it somehow. The great day arrived, and Bob (my brother-in-law) was my best man. As usual with Bob, he was late. He came rushing round sweating like a pig. He said he had got held up at the barbers. Fancy leaving his haircut until the last minute, but as I said before, Bob was like that. We got to the church and waited for Lilian. She looked lovely in a blue dress with a huge bunch of gladioli in her arms. Ever since, by hook or by crook, I have always bought gladioli for Lilian on our anniversary.

Her family gave us a wonderful reception. Considering nobody had much money, we were very fortunate indeed. We never had a honeymoon, our funds would not run to it. I shall never forget the first morning after we were married. As you know, my home life previously wasn't up to much. Lilian woke me up with a cup of tea, and started to get breakfast ready.

I got up, washed and sat down to a lovely breakfast of eggs and bacon, bread and butter and marmalade, all beautifully set out. I thought I was in heaven.

All the following week, not having to go to work, life was bliss. I can honestly say it was the best week of my life. Come the following Monday, I had to get ready to go to work and all the time I was getting ready, we hardly spoke to each other. The thought of having to part for just a few hours seemed like the end of our world. We were nearly in tears as I went off. Lilian waved to me until I was out of sight. That first day at work was the longest day of my life, but it didn't take us long to realise that if I didn't work we couldn't eat.

The following year, our first baby was born. It was a boy, and I felt very proud. Money was short, however, and after a few weeks of my son's birth, we were asked to go and live with Lilian's family. They knew things were bad with us and thought this was an opportunity to get us straight. With much regret, we left our love nest in Tottenham and moved back to Walthamstow. We settled in and all got on very well together, soon working ourselves out of debt and back on our feet.

Meanwhile, Lilian's father retired at 65 years of age. He had worked for a local firm of builders for many years. Some of the joints in his fingers and wrists were crippled after working his whole life out in all weathers. I shall never forget the poor old chap on his last day at work. His mates had put round a subscription list in order to get him a few bob. He brought the list home and I had a look at it. When I looked, I saw the boss's name and the amount he put on the list. It was the princely sum of ONE SHILLING. This was the man who had made a fortune out of the likes of poor old pop. This man also preached from a pulpit in church every Sunday evening.

We had been living with Lilian's dad and brothers for two happy years when Lilian told me she was expecting another baby. We knew it would be impossible in our current circumstances, so we decided to look for another place to live. I got all the papers and tried everywhere I knew, but it was just hopeless. As a last resort I went to a shark agent who offered us two rooms upstairs and one down in an old house. The rent was 15/- per week, which was exorbitant for such a place. Living in the house was a couple with three small children. The woman suffered from fits and the husband was always on the beer. The prospects didn't look good, but we had to take it. Paying 15/- out of £2 7s. 6d. didn't leave much to bring a family up on, so I decided to look for another job. I heard one was going at a firm of clock case makers in Essex Road, Islington. I went and saw them and was given a trial to test my skills as a woodworking machinist.

I proved satisfactory and was given the job at £3 5s. 0d. This was much better money than I had been earning, but the work was much harder. The foreman was a real tyrant. He would walk up and down the lines of machines with his hands behind his back and a scowl on his face. He really kept us at it. When he was tired of walking, he would go to a corner of the shop and stand on a box, watching every movement we made. When a load of timber came in, he would stop all the machines and everyone would have to unload.

Usually it was planks of mahogany, 20 ft long, 18 in wide and 4 in thick. We had to balance these on our shoulders and take them to a cross-cut saw, where they would be cut in half and stacked. After four or five tons of this, our shoulders were raw. We worked from 8 am to 6 pm on weekdays, and to 1 pm on Saturdays. Overtime was worked from September to December at a flat rate.

Just before our second son was born, I had a breakdown with very bad bronchitis. The living conditions and hard work had got me down in the end. My only income was now 15/- per week. This was state sick benefit. As this only paid the rent, I had to apply for public relief. I managed to get to the Relief Office and I had to sit behind a hundred others.

When my turn came for the interview, I was severely reprimanded for not calling the official 'Sir'. I was forced to grovel and apologise. After seeing my marriage papers, birth certificate etc, he granted me 18/- for food. This was given in the form of a ticket that had to be taken to a local shop. This was only after an official had called at my home to verify my statement. He also warned me that if I misappropriated the money in any way I would be liable to legal proceedings and could be imprisoned for same.

My second son was born on the 29th of November, 1929. Looking back on my life, this was the lowest I ever sank. Hardly any of our people could help us as they were all in similar circumstances, but they gave what they could. The day our baby was born, my sister Florrie came with a few things and offered to take the eldest boy back with her for a few days. He was only two years and nine months old, and Florrie loved him. Towards the evening, we both missed him so much that Lilian, amid tears, said she would like him back. I knew that we couldn't go the night without him, so I got ready and went to Florrie's to get him back. I told her the reason why I had come and she understood our point of view. She got him dressed and I cuddled him all the way home. Lilian's face lit up at the sight of him. It was wonderful to see them both. Anyone would think that they had been separated for months. Even if we had nothing, our home was filled with the love we had for each other.

About a week after the baby was born, the insurance man called and gave us £2 maternity benefit. There I was, stony broke with hardly anything in the house by way of food and £2 in my pocket for the doctor and midwife. These two were immediately chased from my mind as I got ready to go out and buy some good food. We lived well for the next week. When the confinement was over, the midwife and doctor asked for the money that I had spent. I told them I would settle up later. I was eventually summoned for the money, which I paid by instalments of 1/6d per week. They accepted, and a debt collector called every Saturday morning for the money.

The awful place we lived was really getting both of us down; it was a normal occurrence to hear the children downstairs screaming as their mother lay on the floor in a fit. We finally decided to look around for another place. One Friday night, we were returning home after a visit to my mother. Glancing in an estate agent's window, we spotted a notice with 'Flats to Let' written on it.

As we had the Saturday morning free, we went in and made enquiries. It was a three-room flat at £1 per week. Although we were finding it hard to pay 15/-, we decided to have a look.

We went and inspected it, deciding we would go back to the agent to see if we could have it. He was a decent sort of chap and hardly wanted to know about references. This suited us fine.

We were already £6 15s. 0d. in arrears and didn't want any enquiry by the landlord. I borrowed the first week's rent from Bob and paid it to the agent. He said I could move in anytime.

Our problem now was how we would pay off the arrears and find the money to move to the new flat. I went to see Bob and we had our usual conference. We decided to do a moonlight flit, and try and raise the money in any way to pay for the removal. The only thing that I had of value was a burr walnut chiming-clock. I had bought it from the firm at cost price of £4, which I used to pay off at 2/ 6d per week. It was worth about £12. I tried many jewellers but could only get an offer of £3. Towards the end of the week I was getting despondent. The removal van was booked and I just did not know where to turn for the money. On the Monday morning I explained to my foreman that I was moving that afternoon and he stretched a point by letting me have the afternoon off without pay. I got home about 2 o'clock and Lilian had everything packed. I thought it only right that I should explain to the tenants downstairs what I was about to do.

After listening to my story they promised they wouldn't let anybody know my future whereabouts, saying they wished they could do the same. The chap (Tom was his name) advised me to take the clock to a pal of his who owned a greengrocers and ask him £5 for it. I went along with the clock under my arm and explained the position. He was a real tough nut. His daughter was getting married and he was looking for a present for her.

He knocked me down to £4, which I was forced to accept. I now had a few bob and was hoping to get out of trouble with my old debts. I went and thanked Tom, giving him half a crown for a drink. I told Lilian my good news and sent her round to the new flat. I waited until it was dark when the moving men arrived. They had strict instructions not to come beforehand. They gave me a hand loading the van and within half an hour we were away.

When we arrived at the flat, Bob was there to give a hand. We unloaded and paid off the removal man with strict instructions not to let anyone know where we were living.

We soon settled down into our home. Somehow our luck seemed to have changed. Work livened up and we were doing overtime. The children had a garden they could play in and we were all very happy. In the summer, we would spend our weekends and holidays at a spot in Epping Forest. Bob and his wife Maud would come round to the flat about 11 o'clock, pack up a load of food for a picnic, and away we would go. Lilian and Maud would get on a tram, while Bob and I would push the pram with the children and the grub in it. It took us an hour, but what's an hour when one is young.

As soon as we arrived, we'd put the kettle on the primus stove and make tea. Out came the grub, and we all tucked in. After, we'd play with the children, climb trees and go exploring. About 6 o'clock, everyone had had enough and we would wend our way home. If we were in funds we'd open a tin of salmon and have a high tea. Looking back, they were happy days. We only wanted the small things in life and most of these were denied us.

One Monday I went to work as usual and was told on arrival that the foreman had got the sack. It just didn't seem possible that this could happen. We were all overjoyed that this tyrant had at last got his deserts. About 9 o'clock, the boss sent in for the senior machinist and asked him to take over the foreman's job. He was an elderly chap and didn't relish the responsibility. A shop meeting was arranged and I was asked to take the job on. I explained to the men that I just could not take this on as tyranny wasn't one of my strong points. An explanation of my refusal was sent in to the office, and I was sent for and asked to reconsider my decision. I explained to the boss that I was not out to make other men's lives a misery and if that was expected of me then count me out. I was coerced into giving it a trial, running the mill as I thought it should be run.

I reluctantly took the job on. I was given a £1 a week rise and all holidays paid for. This was a big inducement, but I wasn't happy. Every one of the chaps promised me their loyal support, and things went very successfully for the first two months.

We were mainly on contract work for a big cigarette manufacturer that gave gifts for coupons. The gifts were clocks we made. We couldn't turn them out fast enough. Three and four hundred a day were our target. Suddenly, out of the blue, Parliament passed a bill making this form of trading illegal. All orders were cancelled and things looked very black indeed. One day I was sent for in the office and the boss told me he had taken on a contract for a mail order firm, which entailed making thousands of striking clocks. I was informed that the cases would have to be made for 3/- each.

I told him that it was almost impossible to make cases of that description for 3/-, but it was either I do them for that price or else. I accepted the challenge although I knew I was fighting a losing battle. I had some fine chaps working for me, with all the loyalty one could desire, but I just could not get down to this ridiculous figure of 3/- a case. After a month of production, my figures were too high. Again I explained the impossibility of such a low figure and was told that if I couldn't do the job someone else would. Next day, to our amazement, the old tyrant was back at his old job. I was told to leave if I wanted to, but if I cared to stay on I could have my old job back.

What could I do? This was 1931 and there were 2 million unemployed. Although I felt humiliated, I had to accept their offer.

The foreman came back a bigger tyrant than ever. He ranted and raved and made our lives a misery, especially mine. He baited me like a cat playing a mouse, waiting for me to slip up. He got me in the end. I came in one morning five minutes late, and that was it, just what he had been waiting for. 'Go in the office and get your cards,' he said. I was in no position to argue and there was nothing I could do. The boss refused to see me and I got the sack. This was my first time out of work since 1924. My only consolation was they went bust a few weeks later.

CHAPTER TWO

I was now signing on at the local Labour Exchange, but there were no jobs to be had so I had to apply for benefit. After giving three days notice, the benefits were as follows:

18/- for myself, 7/- for my wife, and 1/- for each child. This gave me the grand total of 27/- per week. I was forced to apply for public relief.

I got a food ticket for about 18/-, but this only gave us a mere existence. Day after day I walked the district, calling in at all the factories. I would also do a tour of the East End. I knew it was a waste of time but had to satisfy myself that at least I was doing everything I could to find employment.

Eventually, I heard that machinists were wanted at a local firm that made radio cabinets. I went along to make enquiries and saw the foreman who offered me ½d an hour. They made cabinets for most of the leading radio manufacturers and were also making thousands of portable gramophones. The place was stacked from floor to ceiling with work, everyone was falling over each other. The conditions were shocking, but they employed some of the most highly skilled machinists I have ever known. The work had to be fantastically accurate and called for the highest degree of skill. One had to be able to make the saw talk.

On a good week, you could earn somewhere in the region of £3. One can only say that 'it was a job.' That meant something in 1932 and 1933.

If I am going to be honest, I learned more with this firm in two years than I would have learned in ten elsewhere.

Although the work was hard, we somehow managed to have some laughs. There were some weird characters working there.

Sometimes we had to do a night shift and there was one individual who was always good for a laugh. His name was Joe and he was so thin we used to call him 'Splinter.' He was 30 years old and had six children. He took advantage of any spare time he could get to lark about with the women. If a young girl, or any female, walked past him while he was working at his machine his favourite remark was 'I wouldn't arf' like to do 'er.' He always had 'the urge.' Splinter worked a planing machine and opposite him some women operated drilling machines. The planer had a habit of stopping when the board of timber was all but a foot through. To get it through, he had to grip the lower end of the table and force it through with the lower end of his stomach. Splinter was watching the women bending down and could see more than he should have. This gave him a violent 'urge' and he suddenly gave out a terrific yelp.

A couple of us ran over to see what was wrong. It seemed that as he was forcing the plank through the machine, he had caught the tip of his dick on the edge of the table. He was bent over in agony, holding it and screaming. He eventually got it out and it was badly bruised. We took him to the first aid hut, but didn't know how to explain to the woman in charge what he had done. We were killing ourselves with laughter, all except poor Splinter. In the end we explained what happened and got it out for him. The first aid woman bandaged it up and advised him to go to the hospital. Poor Splinter, he never lived it down. It must have been months before he ever got the 'urge' again.

Many accidents happened and were not all comical like Splinter's. Many had badly cut fingers and some were cut off completely. One young chap fell and his arm dropped in the cutters of a planing machine. It was cut to ribbons. Splinters in fingers were the most common occurrence. I have opened many fingers with a sharp knife, removing the splinter immediately, before it turned septic. Most of the accidents could have been prevented, but the operators worked without the guards on the machines because they hampered their efforts to get a living. If word got around that the factory inspector was coming, all guards were put back on quickly. As soon as he went, they would all come off again. It was a rat race to make a living. Nearly everyone was put off a week or two before Christmas, but as soon as trade got going again, we were sent for again.

We lost about three months' time every year. There was another radio factory in the district that always seemed to have enough work without putting off their workers. We all thought that if we could get a job there, we would be set up for good. One day, I met a pal of mine who told me he had heard a job was going there and advised me to apply. I went along, saw them and got the job. I asked for 1s 6d an hour but could only get 1s 4d. The job was operating a belt-sanding machine, which gets the cabinet ready for polishing. It was no easy job. I started in the very busy season and could work round the clock if I wanted to. We were often working until 10 pm or midnight. I wanted the money and was prepared to work for it. Sometimes I only saw the children on Sunday afternoons.

After Christmas we went on normal time, which was 8 am until 6 pm. We were never put off, but sometimes we worked short time if trade slackened. The factory had outgrown itself and the bosses had a new one built. The firm was run by two brothers. They were always rowing and fighting; it was normal to see one chasing the other with a piece of wood in his hand, ready to clout him if he caught him. They often had to be separated.

We eventually moved to the new factory, which was a huge place, all modern with new machinery. Trade was slack and our lives were made a misery. Anyone caught loafing around was sacked on the spot. Bill Frazer, the foreman, made himself look efficient by walking about with a drawing under his arm. He knew as much about reading a drawing as the drawing knew about him, but he was forever picking people's brains and getting the credit for someone else's ideas. Frazer was gambling mad, and if he had given as much time and study to his work that he did on football slips, horses and dogs he would have been a genius.

As time went on the factory got busy, I was put in charge of a line of machines and did my best to get the best out of the chaps. I got a small rise in wages for this, but they would not pay the proper rate to the operators and, consequently, I only got semi-skilled operators at about a shilling an hour. I had to give them the simple part of the job, which made my job harder. They intended to pay for the new factory by getting people working harder but on low wages. This policy eventually made them millionaires.

CHAPTER THREE

We were now into 1935. Although we used to visit our families regularly, we were somehow beginning to drift, as families do. My mother was still living with my sister Florrie, but my younger sister had married and moved away so I didn't see much of her. As for Gerry and Mary, I hardly ever saw them. They were still living in Hoxton. He now had regular work and they lived within their own circle.

The only time we were all together was at reunions, such as Mum's birthday, when we would all have a whip round for drinks and a good old-fashioned party. I was nearly always with Bob. He was mostly at my place. We would try and sort out the world's troubles, and almost everything topical. We had our summer picnics with the children in Epping Forest and life went on.

We were still being driven very hard at work. In 1936, we had secret meetings with those we could trust to see if we could get the firm organised by the trade unions. We managed to get about two dozen chaps in the end. We hired a small hall and invited union officials to come along and give us advice and guidance as to the ways and means of getting the firm organised.

It was decided that the trade union organiser would go to see the bosses to try them out. During the following week the organiser called at the front office, but the bosses refused to see him. He waited until the dinner hour and called a meeting at the factory gates. He told us of the benefits we would get if we joined the union. At our next secret meeting, I was instructed to get up a round robin. This is a sheet of paper with a circle drawn in the centre. Names are added all round the circle. Whoever signed would not be first on the list, so that if anyone was caught they could not be accused of

'heading the list'. We were all equal in our decision to join. I talked
to the chaps about the union whenever I got the chance and by the
Friday of the following week I had a full list of names. Somehow
word got to the foreman Frazer that we were trying to organise the
factory into the trade union, and that I was carrying a list of names
in my pocket. Frazer never had the courage to come and ask if this
was true. He did just what his type would do and went straight into
the office to inform on me. I had a friend in the office who came and
told me what Frazer had done, so I was prepared for what might
happen. Just before knocking off time, one of the bosses came and
poked me hard on the shoulder, demanding to see the list of names.
'What names?' I said.

'You know what bloody names,' he replied. He was going scarlet
in the face. 'I'll have you know, I'll have no bloody trade union here.'

I ignored him and told him I had no names, defying him to find
them. If only he had known it, they were sticking out of my back
pocket. It was a busy time of year and I knew he could not afford to
sack me. As he was bellowing away at me and I treated him with
contempt, the whistle went for knocking off time. His last words as
I was getting ready to go home were that he was going to report me
first thing in the morning.

That night we held our meeting and I presented the organiser
with the round robin. At least we now had something we could
work on. It was agreed that the organiser would call in at the office
again during the following week. I went to work as usual the next
morning and ignored the request for me to report to the office. It
wasn't long before I was sent for along with two others. We were
told by the two bosses that they would rather close the place down
than have the trade union. Again, we denied all knowledge of the
list. I knew he was bluffing with regards to shutting the place down.
We were dismissed and told that the matter would be looked into
further. I was sent for again and given a pep talk. They told me that
my future was assured with the firm, but I didn't care much for my
future as things were.

We were not worried, as we had laid the foundation for the union. It was now up to them. The firm was expanding fast and had about 150 workers.

By December 1936 Lilian and I were expecting our third baby. I was working 70 hours a week. Once our baby was born, we were getting a bit overcrowded in our flat. So I decided I would try and get a house as soon as possible, but all these things took time. One could buy, but I just could not raise the deposit. Any spare time I had was spent at home, because Lilian had a nervous breakdown after the birth of our baby.

1938 was a year of war scares. Bob and I decided to join the Fire Brigade as part-time members. We used to go every Friday night to do our training. We eventually completed our 60 hours' training, becoming fully-fledged auxiliary firemen.

The firm were trying to get government contracts in view of the impending war with Germany. Radio cabinet work was very scarce indeed, and we were only working short time. The firm changed its Italian name as they were afraid of reprisals from the public, which happened to German firms at the outbreak of the First World War. They still wouldn't recognise the union and compromised by paying us Board of Trade rates, but we still went on fighting for trade union recognition, knowing that if War Office contracts came along they would have to accept the trade union. We just had to play a waiting game.

Meanwhile, my family were growing up. I had to do something about a house, which was no easy matter. One Saturday morning, I cycled to Ilford and called at an estate office to enquire if there were any houses for letting. To my utter amazement, the chap in the office (who I knew from some years ago) told me he had a very nice house to let on a new estate. The rent was £1 a week. It was a big jump from 10/-, but I felt I had to take it. Lilian liked it, and we eventually moved in. It was just like heaven to us. We had a lovely garden and the three children soon settled in.

CHAPTER FOUR

We were very busy at the factory in 1939. We had a Government contract for thousands of chairs and were still making radio cabinets.

The August holidays arrived and the firm was having its week-long shutdown. On our last Friday, the boss called us into his office and told us he was going to pay us an extra half week's money as holiday pay. This, he said, could only apply to a few of us. He said he could not afford to pay us a full week's holiday money at the moment but hoped he could in the future. Being grateful for small mercies, I thanked him. This was the first time in my life that I had ever received holiday pay.

This enabled us to have a decent holiday. Going away was out of the question, but we had some wonderful days out and about in Epping Forest. My three boys and I used to roam the forest, play football and have picnics. They were very happy days.

By August of 1939, war was inevitable. I transferred to the Ilford Fire Brigade, yet heard nothing from them regarding mobilisation in the event of war.

Come September, Hitler invaded Poland and we were at war. I reported to the Ilford Fire Brigade but they still had no information regarding my transfer. Bob came to see me and told me to report back to the Walthamstow branch as I hadn't heard anything. I was glad in a way, as it enabled Bob and I to be together again. On September 2nd, we were both taken on as full time members of the Auxiliary Fire Service. We were lined up, inspected by the chief of the Fire Brigade and sent to various sub-stations. I was selected to take charge of a crew owing to my seniority. We were given a pump, equipment and a station at the back of a local radio factory. I just could not get away from radio. I asked permission for Bob to join the crew, which was granted, and he became our official driver.

Meanwhile, there was plenty of upheaval at home. Lilian was going away with the three boys under the Government Evacuation Scheme, yet nobody knew where they were going. They left on a Sunday morning and we were all heartbroken at the parting. My little son was crying his eyes out for his dad, but the two older boys understood the situation. It was a terrible time for us all. I was given night duty with the Fire Brigade, which meant I was alone all day.

As Bob's wife and children were away, he suggested I stay with him at his place. This would save me going home every day to Ilford, so I jumped at the idea. During the first week, the central control of the Fire Brigade took Bob away and placed him at the electricity station. This was a huge operation with six crews, three on days and three on nights. It was a massive defence against the fires that broke out after bombings. I was sorry to lose Bob. Things were not the same without him.

It wasn't long before I was sent for too, told to pack my gear and report to the electricity station. Bob had approached the chief regarding my transfer, who had willingly agreed. All the personnel of the A. F. S. were directed from this station and the officers intended it to be the crack division of the A. F. S.

We were sleeping in a large hall on concrete floors; no chairs, tables or beds. I approached the officer in charge and asked him how on earth he thought we could do 12 and 18-hour shifts under these conditions. He replied that he had tried to get beds and furniture but none were available. I asked if it was possible to get a requisition for some timber, nails and some close-mesh wire. I told him that if he could get these items I could make beds and furniture. He was delighted with the idea and left to make a telephone call. He came running back and told me it had been accepted, and would I give him a list of my requirements. I gave him my list and, true to his word, the materials arrived the next day. I went home to pick up my tools and started to make 18 beds upon my return.

To make the distribution fair, we placed numbers in a hat and drew one for each member of the crew. I was using 2in × 2in timber, and it took me about two hours to make each bed. For mattresses I used the close-mesh chicken wire and staples. Within a week, we each had a bed, a table and forms to sit on to have our meals. The chaps were all grateful for my efforts.

Meanwhile, I received a letter from Lilian. She had been sent to Ipswich. The boys were missing me terribly and my little son was crying all the time for his dad. I felt awful being parted from them. Friday came, and we received our first week's pay from the Fire Service: £2 18. 6d. This was a drastic reduction in wages from the money I was earning at the factory.

After paying the rent and sending some money to Lilian, I was left without a penny. If it hadn't been for Bob I don't know how I would have managed. By the second week I had no money left to pay the rent. I had an interview with the officer in charge and explained my position. He was very understanding and asked me if I would care to move back to the district. He reckoned he could get me a house with a cheaper rent, so I told him I would consider it. Meanwhile, he arranged an interview with the manager of a large housing estate in the district where I was working and I was offered a house at 14/- a week. I accepted and wrote to Lilian to tell her the news.

Bob and I were on our way out with the night crew the following Monday afternoon when who should be walking towards us but Lilian and our three boys. My little son rushed up to me, put his arms around my neck and nearly strangled me. I asked Lilian why she had come home. She explained that she was living in the house of a minister whose wife had been evacuated and there was just no sense staying in a place which wasn't a safe area. I fully agreed with her decision. Separation was not for us anyhow. They agreed to stay at Bob's house and we went home the following morning. Naturally, Bob came with us. We made arrangements to move into our new house the following morning. I was sorry to leave Ilford. It was such a happy house, but we were one of millions of families whose lives had been altered. We soon settled in, with the boys happy that we were all together again. One would have thought we had been separated for a couple of years instead of a couple of weeks.

This was a phoney period of the war and nothing was happening in the firefighting department. My old firm kept asking me to go back to them, which was a great temptation as the money was so much more than what I was earning. One couldn't do much on £2 18s 5d.

I had several clashes with the council about the treatment they doled out to the A.F.S.. On one occasion, we had been on duty from 2 pm on Sunday until 9 am on Monday morning. We were served breakfast which was sent to us from an outside kitchen run by the council. Complaints had been pouring in from the various substations about the quality of the food and the way it was served up. It was always cold by the time we received it.

This particular morning, the breakfast arrived in the canisters. They were stone cold. Upon opening them we found sausages, beans and cold fat. It looked horrible. Someone started to dish it out on plates, but none of us could eat it.

'What the bleeding hell do they take us for?' said one. 'After an 18-hour shift, we are expected to eat this effing mess? Not so bleeding likely.' I looked at my plate and found two rubber rings in with the 'food.' Someone else discovered a piece of string. We decided we would take our breakfast to the chief of the Air Raid Precautions. We put a plate over the food, wrapped it in a piece of cloth and went to the head office. The deputation consisted of Bob, two others and myself. We all marched down the corridor and were stopped by an individual in uniform asking what we wanted. I said I wanted to see the chief. We were told that he would not be able to see us. I told the man in uniform that we were prepared to wait all day if necessary. We then sat down outside his office. Within 15 minutes we were told that the chief would see us.

'Good morning gentlemen,' he said, 'what can I do for you?'

I pushed the plate under his nose and said 'eat that.' When he saw the beans, sausages and fat complete with strings and rubber rings, he said, 'Good God, what a horrible mess.' We gave him a full explanation as to why we were there, telling him that this was the type of thing we were expected to eat after an 18-hour shift. He understood our point, thanked us for bringing it to his attention and promised us that things would improve in the very near future. I am pleased to say that he kept his word. Next morning we were sent eggs and then haddock the morning after. There was a vast improvement from then on, which only goes to show that if one has the courage, injustice can nearly always be set to rights.

My firm were still asking me to go back and many of the A. F. S. were getting their release. I liked the service and was reluctant to leave, but my family commitments had to come first. I consulted Bob and it was agreed that it was the only thing I could do if I wanted to keep my head above water. I went to the firm, telling them I was prepared to come back, and they sent a letter to the A. R. P. appealing for my release. It was granted. My last day as a full-time member of the A. F. S. was sad. The officers called me into the office and told me how sorry they were that I was leaving. Although my militant nature meant that at times I never saw eye-to-eye with them, we nearly always managed to agree to compromise in the end. I told them I would do part-time service (one night a week) and they were happy with this arrangement. Bob stayed on as his circumstances were different to mine. I knew I would miss his company but also that he would be there for us at every opportunity.

I started back at the firm and was asked to train some women to work the saw benches. We had a War Office contract to make ammunition boxes. I was given six new benches, and started to train the women and girls. It was no easy job. Unless the saw is guarded from every angle, it can be very dangerous. So I made up some guards, making the job as safe as possible.

Christmas arrived, and I told the management I could not do the job anymore and I was confident that the women would be able to carry on with minimum supervision. They gave me another job, sorting out any departments that were behind in production. This was more to my liking. So ended 1939.

CHAPTER FIVE

The firm were now very busy on government contracts. They were expanding fast. New bays were being added to the existing ones and extra staff were being taken on. I still held my position of sorting out bottlenecks that held up production. We were not organised in the trade union, yet negotiations were in progress, but without any results.

I was doing part time in the A. F. S. and the phoney war was still going on. It was a bad winter and coal was getting hard to come by. The A. F. S. gave a late Christmas party for the children in a hall which we hired, situated in a deserted school. I took my boys along. We were terribly short of fuel at home and, on arrival, I noticed a great big heap of coal. There must have been about 20 tons of it.

One of the officers arrived with his wife and child at the same time as myself. 'Look at that stack, Harry. I could do with a sack of that at home,' I said to him.

'Don't touch it, Stan,' he replied. 'If anyone caught you, it would be your lot.'

'I suppose so,' I said and left it at that. But during the party, I just could not get that stack of coal out of my mind. So I slipped out when all was quiet and found a sack in a lorry. I filled it and put it to one side. After all, I thought, nobody was going to miss one bag of coal. The problem was how to get it home. When the party was over it had started to snow, and someone suggested we put the children in the lorry along with their parents and drop them off at their homes. Harry lived nearby. His wife and child climbed aboard with my boys, then Harry. 'Hold on,' he said suddenly, 'I forgot the pram.'

'Stop there, Harry,' I said, 'We'll get it on for you.' I asked someone to give me a hand and placed the sack of coal in Harry's pram. Away

we went and I was the first one to be dropped off. You should have seen Harry's face when I got the sack of coal out of Harry's pram.

'Well, I'll be buggered,' he said. 'If that's not the bleeding limit.'

Most of my friends were being called up and the firm didn't seem to be able to get many deferments. I didn't fancy the army and thought that, if I were to be called up, I would volunteer for the Royal Air Force. Bob was still in the A.F.S. and I told him what I intended to do. One Saturday afternoon, we both went to the Romford recruiting centre and I put my name down for the R.A.F. as a carpenter rigger. This was the 1st of February 1940 and I was told that I would be sent for in the near future. Bob was getting fed up with the A.F.S. and had a chance to fulfil his ambition by getting a job with the local council. He started to apply for his release when Hitler's spring offensive started.

The time was now getting near and Bob didn't have his release. He was told that his services were required owing to his knowledge of motors. This answer suited neither Bob nor myself. So we decided to go and see the chief of the A.R.P.. We went to his office but they wouldn't let us see him under any circumstances. We were stumped. Finally we decided to track him to his home. I can't remember how we found out where he lived, but find it we did. It was late at night when we called on him and we had one day to go before the final day for granting releases was up. When we got to his home, we just could not believe it. It was a secondhand wardrobe shop. We thought we had been given the wrong address. We decided to chance it and knocked on the side door. The chief himself answered the door. He asked our reason for calling at such a late hour. We explained that Bob's release notice had been in for a month and of his department's refusal to grant it. We also explained that the next day would be too late and that Bob was within his rights to have his release, even at this late hour. He said he would do what he could the next day. This was not good enough for us. We had to threaten him and he took our threat seriously. Needless to say, Bob got his release from the A. F. S. the next day. There weren't many who managed to pull a fast one on either Bob or myself, although many tried.

As Hitler's offensive got going, I was called up for a trade test by the R. A. F.. I arrived at Cardington about 4pm. It was a huge camp with a turnover of a thousand recruits a day. We were given a medical examination upon arrival and told the trade test would take place the next day. We were also told that we would be able to return home afterwards to get our affairs in order and be called up at a later date. Next morning, after breakfast, we were lined up and taken to various clerks who were sitting at tables in a large hall. On this day, the evacuation of Dunkirk had started.

Panic broke out at Cardington and huge notices were chalked up on the wall that read 'VACANCIES WERE IMMEDIATE.' This meant there was no going home to put our affairs in order. There would be no trade test until after we were sworn in. Hundreds went in front of the clerks signing forms for enrolment, being sworn in irrespective of trade or profession. My turn came, and I was told by an arrogant clerk to sign the form and be sworn in. I told him in no uncertain terms that I had come here of my own free will and, unless I could be enrolled as a carpenter-rigger, I wouldn't sign up.

'You'll do as I tell you,' he said. 'Sign and wait your turn.' This got my back up, as I knew he couldn't do this to me. This can only happen after one is sworn in. The clerk was losing his temper with me. 'Go and sit over there and I'll see about you later,' he said.

I sat and waited for over an hour, when a corporal came up and asked me what the trouble was. I gave him a full explanation as to what had transpired between myself and the clerk. On hearing this, the corporal congratulated me on knowing my rights.

'Sit in my office, Mr Jasper,' he said, 'I'll go round the camp and see if there is a vacancy in your trade.' I shall never forget that corporal. He was one of the nicest individuals I had ever met. He came back after half an hour and apologised for keeping me waiting. He told me that he had been all over the camp but there were no vacancies for my trade. He suggested I go home for the time being and as soon as a vacancy was available he would let me know. He took me to a clerk who paid me two days' money and a ticket home. The clerk asked me for my identity number and those of my wife and children, as well as their ages and dates of birth. I gave him all the details from memory without referring to any papers in my pocket. The clerk was amazed: 'Most of them that come in here don't even know their own birth date, let alone their families'' as well.' I got on very well with him and he said I was doing the right thing. He said most of the others were 'just like a load of sheep.' I thanked the clerk and the corporal and made my way home. I was the only one that came out of Cardington camp that day, simply because I knew my rights. I knew I would be more use to the R. A. F. following my trade and not doing some other menial job.

The next day I started work at the factory again, informing them that I could be called up again at any time in the near future. They promised me a deferment but I told them I wasn't interested.

The bombing had now started in earnest. Towards the end of the year I was having trouble with a cartilage in my knee and had to have three weeks off from work, as it had swollen up like a balloon. I eventually went back to work near the end of the year.

The doctor ordered me into hospital for an operation. I hated the idea of leaving the family, especially while the bombing was going on, but it was imperative I had the operation. My wife came to visit afterwards with only two of the boys. She claimed that he was staying with his friend. I could not believe this; I knew my boy would not stay away from me just to be with his friend. Eventually, she told me the truth. I had only been in hospital four days when my son had the most terrible accident. He was playing in the street and his ball went into a front garden. He climbed over the iron rails, slipped, and impaled himself on the spike of one of the railings. The poor kid, he nearly lost his life. How my wife survived the worry of both of us being in hospital, I will never know.

She had to visit me in one hospital and my son in another. I discharged myself after two weeks. I simply had to get home and shoulder some of the responsibilities. In the end, my son had to have three operations and eventually got better, but it was touch-and-go for a time.

I never went back to my old job. I sent a letter to the firm asking for my insurance cards. These were eventually sent to me, and I hoped that this would be the last time I ever went near the place again. I had a good knowledge of carpentry and a set of tools. I thought I would try my hand as a carpenter. I got a job with a small builder and got on very well. I liked the life. It was such a change from being stuck inside a factory. I was still doing part time in the A.F.S. I got on very well with lads and we had many a get-together at our home. It only took the slightest excuse for a party to be arranged. Many's the time there were three fire engines parked outside our house with a good old ding dong going on inside.

In 1942, I was sent for by the Ministry of Labour. I was told that I would have to take up my trade again as a machinist. I was directed to an aircraft factory. It was a massive place with hundreds working there. I had to work a two-shift system, 8am to 7pm and a 7pm to 7am night shift, but the money was good.

I was in my element. They had some wonderful machines and I enjoyed finding out how they all worked. Before the war, this factory made mass-produced furniture. Their operators only knew mass-production methods, but aircraft was a different kettle of fish. They were simply lost when it came to precision woodwork. Having had good training, I soon settled in and was accepted into the trade union. It wasn't long before I became shop steward. I had to listen to all sorts of grievances and complaints. Some were justified but most were of a petty nature.

I attended production meetings and was kept very busy. I had to give up going to the A. F. S.. I received a letter from them asking me why I had given up my part-time service. I replied, telling them of the trouble I was having with my leg and how I would be hampered if I had to attend a fire. I was told to attend a medical examination, which I did. The doctors found me to be unfit for duty and I was given my discharge, but I was sorry to sever my happy association with them.

Women were now being directed into industry and working on aircrafts. This caused quite a stir amongst the men, who refused to help train them. Shop meetings were held and, in the end, we had to compromise by having them 'pull out' from the back of the machines. This was usually done by a lad who was learning the trade. Many of the old hands still refused to have women on their machines but I saw nothing wrong with having the women assisting and I said so. The only way was to set an example. I had a word with the shop foreman and offered to take the first woman on the back of my machine. Being a shop steward, I had to put up with jeers and insults over this but I carried on.

In 1943, the firm were making 'Mosquito' aeroplanes, and I was asked to set up a new department. The idea was to get a good production going with machined parts, ready for the women to start assembling.

The working hours were long. Sometimes I left for work at 7.30 in the morning and didn't arrive home until 7.30 the following night. This happened whenever we had a night fire-watching. If we were on a night shift, we all looked forward to Sunday morning which then meant we were off for two days. Working 60 or 70 hours per week took some doing. During the bombings we worked until the last few seconds of the warning which proved to be very trying.

CHAPTER SIX

The factory was employing women in hundreds of different jobs which entailed a vast increase in the numbers employed.

Our dinner break on the night shift was 12.30 to 1.30 am and on a summer night we would go for a stroll outside after we had finished our meal. There would be several couples standing against the wall, kissing and cuddling. Some of these men I knew personally and most of them were married.

The personnel office became overworked with enquiries from the wives of men who worked there regarding their carryings-on with various women. One night, I was discussing the subject with the shop manager and, after our meal, he invited me to go for a walk to one of the shops where the planes were being assembled. It was pitch dark except for two pilot lights.

'Watch this,' he said suddenly. He switched on all the lights and couples came in to view from all directions, mostly with their clothing disarranged. It had to be seen to be believed and the management was pressed to do something about it. They eventually did, after the following incident.

We had a junior personnel officer and part-time member of the works fire brigade who fancied himself with the women. Regarding his firefighting qualities, he was useless. It seemed he was always missing when it was his night on duty. The fire brigade chief kept an eye on him and was determined to find out what he was up to. One night, after trying to find him in all the most likely places, the chief decided that the only other place was the personnel office. Gently trying the door, he found it to be locked. So he went to the front office and asked for the duplicate key, which the night security man gave him. The chief got another man to go with him as a witness. They carefully opened the door and went straight into the inner office. There was the personnel officer with a girl on the couch, half undressed. When challenged as to what they were up to, he made out they were practising first aid. He was sent for the following morning by the board of directors and sacked on the spot.

The factory had a bomb disposal unit within the home guard, and I was asked to join. This would mean attending a two-hour lecture once a week, together with parades on a Sunday morning. This, in turn, meant that I would be exempt from all night fire-watching, so I decided to accept. I attended the lectures and helped dig out many dummy bombs. It wasn't too bad. They were a decent lot of chaps, mostly from the engineering section of the factory. Towards the end of 1942, a big second front meeting was to be held at Earls Court and I was asked to go as a delegate, make a report, and report back to our union branch.

Heading a line of Russian delegates was the famous Red Army sniper, Lyudmila Pavlichenko. A crowd of 10,000 stood up and cheered this amazing woman for three full minutes. Following was Lieut. Pochlinsev, also a hero of the Red Army, with 150 German soldiers to his credit. Another notable delegate was Krassavchenko, head of the Soviet youth movement.

The Mayor of Fulham took the chair, addressing us all as Comrades and Friends. He told us how the Soviet Union had grown in the past 25 years, how it was feared by enemies and loved by friends. To the Russian delegates he said, 'We salute you, comrades, for the valour and bravery shown by the Red Army, Navy and Air Force.' At the conclusion of his speech, he said 'Let us see that in the future, relations with the Soviet Union remain unbroken and plan together for a better world.' Loud cheers greeted him.

From the writers and film workers of the Soviet Union came the message that they were 'confident that Britain and Russia, fighting on two fronts, will rout the German beasts to final victory. Long live the unshakeable unity between the United Nations and the U.S.S.R.'.

The Mayor of Fulham next called on Lieut. Lyudmila Pavlichenko to speak. Amid a battery of photographers and tumultuous cheering, she rose and gave her speech in Russian. It was translated into English afterwards. She began with 'greetings to all the people of Great Britain from all the people of the Soviet Union, the Red Army, Navy and Air force. When Hitler's hordes started war with Russia,' she went on, 'he did not realise the Russians could withstand the full weight of Germany.'

She told us how the Red Army were grateful for the tanks made by the workers of Britain, delivered by the glorious Merchant Marines and the Royal Navy. But that help, she said, 'was insufficient on its own because the war demanded more sacrifices. Our strength lies in this, that we are fighting for the liberation of Europe, for the smashing of fascism and complete victory for the United Nations.' Again, the whole crowd of ten thousand people got to their feet and cheered.

Professor Casine spoke next for France. He told us how, from 1917 onwards, the capitalist countries had tried to split the workers of the U. S. S. R.. He was loudly applauded at the conclusion of his speech. An impressive military display preceded Stalin's speech, which was read by Joseph Macleod of the BBC, and received with the greatest show of applause I have ever heard.

Isabel Brown next took the platform. What a wonderful speaker this woman was. She told of how the men and women of Britain were inspired by the gallant Eighth Army, and how she hoped that this was only a forerunner of what was going to happen in the future. It was interesting that she gained more applause than any other speaker.

To conclude, I wish to add that I am in full agreement with Isabel Brown's words: 'Let us stand with applause for our wonderful allies. Let us see that every one of us set our hearts to the task of bringing utter defeat to the filthy system of the so-called New Order and complete victory for the United Nations.'

The account of this rally took place when the Soviet Union was looked upon as a valuable ally. Nobody then was aware of the atrocities carried out by Stalin either during the war or before the war started.

CHAPTER SEVEN

The end of November 1943 found me suffering from a severe attack of bronchitis. The dust from the machines and the synthetic glue we were using didn't help. I was forced to go to the Manor House Hospital to undergo tests. X-rays showed I had a spot on my lung and I was warned by the specialist that unless I gave up my present job, it would get worse. I felt very reluctant to do this as I liked my work but common sense prevailed. I decided to take the specialist's advice. He gave me a letter which I had to give to my personnel officer. He offered me a job on the airfields but this would mean living away from home, and I needed special food and attention which I could only get at home. The firm had been very good to me and I left reluctantly. They gave me a bonus and told me that, should my health improve, the door was always open to me.

I was in a quandary as to what to do. There was only one trade that would help me to regain my health, which was the building trade. After a month's rest, I got a job with a small builder by the name of Trevor. He was repairing bomb-damaged houses but only had a small staff. I took a job as a carpenter and my health showed signs of improvement after a while. It wasn't long before I had to submit myself for a medical examination by the doctor of the Home Guard.

I had to see a doctor in Wood Green, who at first treated me as though I was a malingerer. After his examination, he tendered me his sincere apologies. He told me that so many men were trying to take him on for their discharge. He sent his report to the district office of the Home Guard and I was given my discharge. I was told at the same time to hand in all my equipment and uniform to the depot at Muswell Hill. I couldn't manage all of this alone, so I asked Bob to give me a hand.

We arrived at the depot about 7pm and were confronted by a big
bully of a man.

'You're too bleeding late to hand it in mate, come back another
time and make it early.' I told him he wasn't talking to some poor
little rookie and, if he didn't take it, I was going to bleeding well
leave the stuff outside his door. It was the only language an ignorant
brute like him could understand. He still refused to take my stuff
in, so I just slung it at his feet and walked away. He called me back
and gave me a receipt.

Sam Trevor, my boss, now had more work than he could cope
with. I asked him why he didn't hire more men so that we could get
on with the job. His reply was that he had only ever been a small
builder and had no desire to employ a larger workforce. The council
were beginning to chase him as he was getting so far behind and
something had to be done. I offered to take over the foreman job
and try and find some more labour.

He agreed to this as there was no alternative. I started to make
some order out of his chaos, managing to find a bricklayer and a
couple of labourers. This brought our staff up to seven. I tried all
the labour exchanges and got the same reply. They said they would
see what they could do, but nothing ever came of it. I happened to
mention this to George the bricklayer, as he was a chap who knew
his way around. He told me I was going about it the wrong way and,
if I would like to go for a drink in a certain pub one night, he would
introduce me to a Ministry of Labour official, who said that he could
get all the men I wanted at the cost of one pound a time. I just could
not believe this kind of corruption existed. I explained it to Trevor
and told him we had to have more men if we wanted to compete
with other firms. Now was the time to take a chance and expand the
business. He gave me ten pounds and told me to go and see what I
could do. He really didn't want to know about it.

I arranged to meet George that night. I arrived about 8pm and
he was already there. We were having a drink when in came the
man from the Ministry. 'Good evening, George,' he said and invited

me to have a drink. They were both long-standing drinking pals. I was asked what type of labour I required. I told him and handed him the ten pounds. He told me my requirements would be met and after a while I left. True to his word, I had three carpenters, two slaters and tilers, two plasterers and three labourers by the end of the week. We were now able to get the job going. The council officials came along and saw the progress we were making, recognising me as the general foreman.

I asked Trevor what he thought about getting some more men, telling him I had to have at least 30. He gave me a free hand but all this talk terrified him and he didn't want to know any details. He seemed quite satisfied to sit back and take 15% commission on labour and materials. I got him to give me another twenty pounds, and that night I went to the same pub to have another meeting with the man from the Ministry. I passed over the money, stated my requirements and left. During the next few days, all my requirements were met. This was my first experience of graft and corruption but it wouldn't be my last.

As time went on, we were getting quite a good name in the borough for getting the job done. Anybody who was anybody in public life, such as councillors or even the local M P who had been bombed out, sent for me via the war damage officer and had me repair their houses. The reason given to me as to why these jobs were passed to me was that I 'could do the work like a diplomat.' In other words, 'give them what they want but don't let others know.'

It was heartbreaking to see the conditions people were living under after they had been bombed out. Many's the time that, after a raid, we worked late into the night putting up tarpaulin on a roof to save the family getting flooded if it rained. More than once I had a complete road of houses finished and was ready to start on another road, when a rocket would drop in the vicinity and we would have to go back and start all over again. Trevor was still keeping in the background, leaving everything to me. I wasn't getting much out of all this extra work, just about a pound more than any of the craftsmen I employed. I was continually being offered other jobs. Builders used to ask me how I managed to get such a large staff. Would I care to start for them and name any figure?

I tackled Trevor and told him of the offers I was getting, and that I wasn't satisfied with my lot. After all, he had never had it so good and it was mainly due to my efforts. He invited me to his house for a discussion. It didn't take long to see who was running his business. Poor Trevor, his wife ruled him with a rod of iron. It was pathetic to see him ask her permission to grant me a quarter of a share in the profits. She said as far as she was concerned it was okay but it would have to be done legally and their solicitor would have to be consulted. I agreed but knew she was stalling for time. I was disgusted with her. Time went on and nothing more was said about my share of the profits. To keep me quiet he would often drop me a quid but that wasn't anything close to what I was supposed to be getting.

I got notice to go for a medical board for the armed forces. I had to report to Romford on the day of days, June 6th 1944; D-Day, the invasion of allied troops into Normandy. I told Bob about it, and he said he would arrange a day off and come with me. I said I would go on my own, but he wouldn't hear of it. He told his employers some tale about a favourite aunt of his who had died and got the day off. I had to be at Romford by 11am. The medical board consisted of five or six doctors in separate cubicles. It was headed by the chairman of the board who sat in the middle of the hall and had the last word on any matter, such as advice to the man who was being examined or to the doctor who had a query.

I stripped off my clothes and was told to sit and wait my turn. I was eventually called and went into the first cubicle. I was told to lie flat, and the doctor started bending my knees so that they nearly touched my chin. As he started to bend my left knee, I told him to go easy as I'd had an operation on my knee. 'It shouldn't hurt after two years,' he said.

'What it should do and what it shouldn't do are two different things,' I replied, 'it hurts, and that's all there is to it.' He could see

I was wearing an elastic knee band but still would not believe me.

Next I had my eyes tested and so on until I came to the last one. He asked me the same stupid question: 'Has there been anything wrong with you lately?' I told him the same as I had told the others, that I had an operation on my knee and a spot on my lung. He thought I was kidding him. 'I can't see anything wrong with your chest now,' he said. He got upset when I asked him if his eyes and ears were equal to an x-ray. When he had finished I was told to wait outside until I was called. By this time he was in a right temper. I sat outside on a chair opposite the chairman's desk. I distinctly heard this last doctor go up to the chairman, saying that there was nothing wrong with me and that I was trying to pull a fast one. 'Alright you bastard,' I thought. 'I have told the truth and now I'll prove it.' The chairman called me to his desk and said 'sit down' in his bulldog way.

'What's all this I hear that you are supposed to have something wrong with your knee and a spot on your lung?' He said. 'Don't come up here telling us a pack of lies hoping to get away with it. It's proof we want.'

I was now all worked up for a fight. 'Proof?' I said. 'If it's proof you want, take a look at this lot.'

I got out my wallet and presented him with the letter from the specialist at the Manor House Hospital. 'Here's my discharge from the fire brigade and my discharge from the Home Guard,' I said, 'Do you want any more bloody proof?' He read each document and was steadily going purple in the face.

'Go and get dressed, and wait outside,' he said. Bob was waiting for me.

'Never mind mate,' he said, 'as soon as you get your card, we'll go and have a nice pint.'

The chap who was next after me came out. 'You ain't 'arf caused a bleedin' row in there mate,' he said. 'After you were told to get dressed, the chairman chewed the balls off the last doctor who saw you.'

I laughed like hell. 'Serves him right. He wanted the truth and he got it.' Soon after, a clerk came out and called my name. I was given a green card which stated 'Grade 4 Unfit.' Needless to say, Bob and I had our pint and a few more, joined by a party of Marines who were on their way to Normandy.

CHAPTER EIGHT

I wasn't getting very far in my partnership with Trevor, so I decided I would risk a showdown. Before I got a chance to tackle him, he told me he had been approached by a neighbour, an electrician by trade, who had money to invest for a partnership in his building business. He reckoned that if I approached the right people in the war damage department, there would be a wonderful opportunity for us to get electrical contracts that were being given out. I asked him where I stood in all this and he said I would be looked after. He promised me he would not go back on his word. He arranged a meeting with the three of us, and I was introduced to a Mr Jim Devinish who seemed a pretty tough guy and who knew all the answers. The proposition put forward was that they be equal partners. This completely left me out in the cold. I told them I didn't like it as far as I was concerned and offered to resign on the spot. I had plenty of other offers in the pipeline and I wasn't worried too much.

Being easy, I was eventually coerced into staying on with them and thought there wasn't anything to lose by giving it a chance. Devinish was a qualified electrician and I asked the war damage officer to give us a trial for any future work that should come along. I was well-known to him and he promised he would help in any way he could. Within a few weeks Devinish was given a contract and he soon had a couple of pairs out working.

I don't know what wages Trevor and Devinish were taking but within a few months Trevor's wife was interfering, telling him he was getting a bad deal. Poor Trevor, I felt sorry for him. He was treated like a little boy at home. He asked me round to see if I could talk to his wife, but as soon as I got there she started ranting and raving. She even accused me of being on the opposite side. In the end, she told me to 'get out and stay out.' I told both of them that this suited me fine and asked for my cards to be made up next morning. Meanwhile Devinish, who only lived opposite, came in just as I was going and told Mrs Trevor to 'mind her own bloody business.' Poor Trevor was shivering in his shoes. After all, he was the most inoffensive chap and just could not stand rows.

I went to work next morning and Trevor asked me to see the week out, offering me his sincere apologies for his wife's outburst. I promised to work the week, and soon after Devinish came and told me he was dissolving his partnership with Trevor. He wanted to see me at my home that night as he had a proposition to put to me. Meanwhile, I explained confidentially to two of my chaps that I would be leaving at the end of the week owing to troubles with the governors, hoping they would keep it to themselves for the time being. Within hours the rumour got round to all the men, who threatened to leave if I did, but I explained to them that no useful purpose would be served by their action, and they agreed to leave the matter in abeyance.

I hadn't been home long before Trevor and his wife called. I asked them in and she offered me profuse apologies for her conduct the night before, asking me to reconsider my decision to leave. They told me Devinish was pulling out and, when everything was settled, I would get my quarter share in the business. I refused point-blank and told them they'd had all the time in the world to do something for me. In any case it was too late. They saw I was adamant and left.

They hadn't been gone long before Devinish called. His proposition was to start a small electrical business and woodworking mill. I had no money to invest and told him so. He suggested he put up the money and pay me so much a week, 50% of the profits and a full partnership at a later date. I agreed as I had nothing to lose but I couldn't make up my mind. I told him I would give it consideration and let him know later. I talked the matter over with Bob and he told me to give it a trial, so I told Devinish I would accept his offer and resigned at the end of the week. Several of the men left with me. I felt sorry for Trevor but he'd had his chance and failed. He only wanted to be in a small way and he reverted to that shortly after I left him.

I spent the next two weeks finding electrical work for Jim Devinish and landed a contract to repair all the seating in a local cinema. We also got premises. Devinish had the upper half and I had the ground floor. I repaired the cinema seats in the mornings and worked in the mill in the afternoons. We bought two or three machines and started to advertise for work. The mill side of the business was slow to get off, so I suggested we make occasional furniture. This required a licence. I made an application to the Board of Trade and sent my discharge papers from the Fire Brigade. I was granted a licence and we got going.

Devinish formed a registered business and called it J. D. & J. Manufacturing. It had our full address and, in very small letters, 'J. Devinish, Prop.' He saw that I looked astonished as I was reading the letterhead, explaining that 'it had to be done from a point of law,' but he would have it altered as soon as he formed a Limited Company. From then on I distrusted him.

'Surely I haven't fallen in it again with false promises?' I thought. I had to let it go, taking a chance with how it would turn out later. I started making small tables, cosmetic boxes, biscuit barrels, etc and took them to the big stores. I got lots of orders. I was now doing all the machining and cabinetmaking, and it was tough going. I had a couple of women polishers, but my own work was too much. Devinish saw this and proposed taking on a cabinetmaker. He said he knew of one and would go and see him. He was a chap who had made a lot of money during the war making black market furniture. He saw how busy I was and thought he was on to a good thing. He and Devinish had a talk in private, and it was suggested to me later that we take him in as partner. His name, by the way, was Tom Tyler. The terms suggested were half-share for Devinish, quarter-share for Tyler and the other quarter-share for me. I could not oppose

Devinish. True, I had laid the foundations of a good business but I owned nothing. It all belonged to Devinish.

The figure Tyler agreed to give, coming into the business, was £500. I accepted as there was nothing else I could do. Tyler paid his money in and started work on a salary and profit-sharing basis. We got on alright. He did the making and I did all the machining. After a week, Devinish called me into his office and told me he was going to make the business into a Limited Company. We were each to be issued with one share to start with. My half of the £500 Tyler had paid in would be split as follows: £125 to be paid into the company for my one share, the other £125 to be given to me minus part of the legal costs. I finished up with about £80. I knew I was getting a bad deal but there was nothing I could do about it. We now had a salesman and work was rolling in. By early 1947 we were well established.

Again, I was to suffer a serious setback. My chest was playing up again and I had to spend about three weeks in bed. They called in now and then to see me and, on more than one occasion, I was asked if I thought I would be able to carry on. I told them I had every hope for the future and would be back as soon as possible. After the third week I felt well enough to go out. I explained their fears to Bob and he suggested we see what had been going on. It was a Sunday evening. I had my own keys but when I tried to open the door I found to my amazement that the locks had been changed. We were both dumbfounded. I couldn't rest and went to the firm the next morning to see what it was all about. Tyler was surprised to see me.

'I didn't expect to see you, Stan,' he said.

'I don't suppose you did,' I replied, and asked him where Devinish was. He told me I would find him upstairs but I wasn't happy with the atmosphere.

I saw Devinish, who shook hands with me and said 'How nice to see you, Stan.' I told him of my experience with the lock and he looked very sheepish: 'I had to change them, Stan, owing to the local burglars being busy in the neighbourhood.' I replied that I didn't believe him and wanted to know why I hadn't been informed. We parted on bad terms. Before leaving, I told him that it was my licence that enabled the firm to keep going and that if there was any funny business I would withdraw it. But he insisted that it was the property of the Company and there was nothing I could do about it.

This was the end as far as I was concerned. I had got myself mixed up with two villains, and after all my hard work was again left high and dry with nothing. I had to get another job. As soon as I was well enough, I contacted the man from the Ministry of Labour and told him of my predicament. 'Don't worry, old man,' he said, 'we can soon get you fixed up.' He gave me a card and a recommendation to take to Woodford Council for a vacancy that was going for a 'Clerk of Works.' I was given an immediate interview and told to start the following Monday.

Meanwhile, I had to do something about Devinish and Tyler. Bob and I had our usual conference, and a course of action was decided on. Firstly, to go to the Board of Trade and discover the position regarding my licence. Secondly, to go to Somerset House and see if I was still on record as Director of the Company. I reversed this order and went to Somerset House first. I paid my shilling to look at the Articles of the Company. True enough, my name had been withdrawn and another inserted. My hunch was right: I had been worked out.

I went next to the Board of Trade. I explained my predicament to a very sympathetic lady who, after hearing my story, told me to wait and she would do her best to get me an interview with the official who had granted the licence. She was gone quite a while and I didn't expect to see anyone that day but, much to my surprise, she came and told me that the official would receive me. I was taken into a very large and elaborate office. The official had been well informed as to my visit by the lady who first saw me. He simply asked me the firm's telephone number. After he got the number, the following conversation took place:

'This is the Board of Trade here, can I speak to Mr Jasper?' Tyler answered the phone.

'I am very sorry sir, but Mr Jasper is out,' was his reply. 'I'll get Mr Devinish, he will probably be able to tell you where he is.' On comes Devinish.

'I am sorry sir, but Mr Jasper is out on business for the firm and is not expected back today.'

'Why all the lies?' said the B.O.T. official.

'This is no lie, sir,' said Devinish, 'Mr Jasper is a very important member of the firm, and spends most of his time on the road getting orders.'

'I guess he is important,' said the B.O.T. official. 'So important that I have him sitting here next to me. I have been listening to his story and I must tell you, you have gained his licence under false pretences. I can give you 24 hours in which to return it, otherwise we will take the necessary steps for its return.'

And with that the B.O.T. official put down the phone. 'This should clear matters up for you, Mr Jasper, and don't get yourself involved with rogues like that in the future.' I thanked him sincerely and he promised he would let me know when the licence was returned. I could imagine them at the other end of the line, and the cocksureness of Devinish, who had told me that 'the licence belongs to the firm.' They must have been shattered.

I started work for Woodford Council as Clerk of Works. It was mainly war damage rebuilding. I was given an office and was available to members of the public from 9 until 10 o'clock each morning. After 10, I had to do the rounds, supervising the local builders. Most of the builders were in a small way and were always ready to 'give a drop' if I would shut my eyes to their shoddy work. I wasn't very popular as I would have none of it. There were five or six of us, and graft and corruption was the order of the day. Most of the clerks would return about 3 o'clock every day, half drunk. They had probably spent two or more hours in the pub with some local builder who had been gearing them up.

One day, I had to keep an appointment with an assessor from the War Damage Commission who wanted to verify a claim. I went on the job with him and during our conversation he asked me why I didn't apply for a job with the War Damage Commission. I told him I would think about it. The longer I left it, the more experience I was getting. In September, I took a course in costing and surveying at the local technical college. I rather fancied working as assessor for the War Damage Commission, but was determined to get as much knowledge as I could before applying. I eventually applied in November and my application took six weeks before I was accepted. I shall always remember the day I got the letter to start: Christmas Day, 1947. Bob and I drank to my success. At last, I had got the position in life that I had been striving for.

CHAPTER NINE

I started working for the War Damage Commission in the first week of January 1948. I had to attend a school in Leadenhall Street and I felt a bit shaky at starting. This was a branch of the civil service and it was my first encounter with the red tape we hear so much about. There were about 40 of us in class, which included ten ex-colonels and two brigadiers who had been demobbed from the Royal Engineers. We were given problems on paper. We had to break each item down and arrive at a figure that was representative of the prices of labour and materials. I got very friendly with one or two of the chaps, but some were snobs who, if successful in the course, would make really arrogant civil servants. Yet I felt sorry for the ex-officers; the poor chaps never had a clue. They may have been used to making roads and building bridges but didn't know the first thing about house repairs, factory repairs and rebuilding.

After a week, I was given my first assignment. I knew this was the start of a series of test assignments and was determined to make a success of it. My first call was an old house in Limehouse. The builders had done the war damage repairs and had been paid. It was the shabbiest job I had ever seen. I made my report, giving my opinion of the poor workmanship and the excessive price charged, but it was like locking the stable door after the horse had bolted. I handed in my report that night and was given another job to assess in Brick Lane. It was a secondhand clothes shop owned by a Jewish occupant. After surveying the place, I came to the conclusion that the damage was 90% dilapidation and 10% war damage. The old chap was trying to claim for a complete rebuild. I explained that this could not be granted as the place was too old. He tried every way to get me to agree, even to the extent of offering me money. I refused point-blank and told him so. This was a bad start to my new job but I wasn't taking any chances. I had heard of one or two cases where assessors had been trapped and caught taking bribes, so I told the old chap I would do what I could for him and asked where the bus stop was. He offered to walk with me to the bus stop and, as the bus came along, I shook hands with him, again telling him I would do my best. As the bus moved off, he ran after me and put something in my pocket. When I sat down, I found it to be a pound note. This got me worried. Should I report it?

'On second thoughts,' I said to myself, 'he may have done it with all good intent.' I didn't want to get the old chap in trouble as he was old, so I had to take a chance. I made my report and stated that 'although the house and shop are old, the life span would have been much longer had it not been for blast from a local bombing incident.' I advised 60% payment towards costs. I never saw this old chap again and I trust he took my offer when it was submitted to him.

I was now getting towards my second week and was given an assessment to carry out at Clapton. This was a furniture shop that had been badly damaged. I prepared a bill of quantities and made a drawing of the proposed shop front. The owners agreed with my assessment and plans, and I submitted my report to my chief. The next day I was sent for, told I had done very well and that the panel of officers were satisfied with my work. I was offered an appointment at Ilford, which I agreed to take. I left Leadenhall Street to start my new job on the following Monday. I made myself known to the chief assessor, who was a permanent civil servant. His job was to act as advisor for anything of a delicate nature. He also had the last word on any dispute between assessor, builder and owner of premises involved. I was given an office and stacks of files relating to various cases of bomb damage that were waiting to be cleared up.

On looking through the files, I discovered that they were mostly awaiting agreement on price before the builders started. I soon started to make a clearance of these files. With some I got full agreement among the concerned parties and, when no agreement could be reached with others, the files were referred to the chief assessor whose word was final. Needless to say, he nearly always gave way to the builder or the claimant as he didn't want any trouble with head office.

This made our work a waste of time. I told him so on one occasion and his reply was 'do it the civil service way boy, we steer clear of trouble then.' This was all very well but we were dealing with thieves and rogues. The head office knew what was going on. The chief was getting nasty official notes to the effect that he was too lenient in most cases and an example was to be made of any future cases of attempted fraud. I was one of two who were detailed on special assignments where deliberate fraud was suspected to be taking place. I started to unmask these rogues and gave each completed case to the chief, complete with evidence, for the attention of head office. These were vetted and if I had proved my point I had the full backing of the chief.

Nothing was ever heard of these cases again. They were either pigeonholed or paid in full to cover up the scandal that was going on. It looked as though the builders and owners were winning. We were getting fed up with seeing our hard work wasted and on more than one occasion I had a case come back from head office, telling me to pay the claim in full with no explanation as to why.

Meanwhile, Bob and I had our weekly get-together. I was always telling him that if I had enough money, I would start on my own again in the woodworking trade. Bob was keen for me to have a go and he said he would see what capital he could arrange. His wife's brother Bert was a good joiner and was also keen to start on his own. Bob suggested he go and see him to arrange a meeting between the three of us.

Back at my office, I was assigned a very nasty case of alleged fraud by a well-known builder. I could see weeks of work ahead. The firm never knew I was investigating them, they were pressing for payment for hundreds of pounds. First, I arranged with their architect to view the work that had been done and during the course of the meeting, they tried all sorts of suggestions, which in plain language meant bribes. When the meeting was over, I started to put the heat on. I checked every bill from different merchants and found most of them had been altered. One item I remember quite well. It was for one ton of cement. I was suspicious of it and went to the merchant concerned, showing him my warrant to inspect his books. I asked to see invoices of the date concerned and what was sold. The invoice was traced and, true to my suspicions, it was for '2 gutter bolts, 4d.' This was an open-and-shut case of fraud.

When I had the case completed, I thought I would give the firm a chance to come out in the open. I approached them with my findings and told them that if they admitted their guilt it would save a prosecution. They saw my point and admitted a grave mistake had been made. They would accept 50% of the original claim as payment in full.

Within a week, they refuted their signed statement and said it had been made under pressure from me. So I made out my case of deliberate fraud with all the evidence at my disposal. Meanwhile Bob, his brother-in-law Bert and myself agreed to start our own business. They would provide the capital and stay at work until the business got on its feet. I was to resign from the War Damage Commission, try to find premises and get it started.

I was given an assessment on a war damage claim with the firm, Stock Ltd. My appointment was fixed for the next day. I met Mr Stock, and, after agreeing to his claim, mentioned I was looking for premises to start a woodworking business. He said he had just the place, and would I care to have a look at it. He was very helpful. I saw the workshops and agreed to take them. I told Bob and Bert the good news and a meeting for the following Saturday was arranged at my house. During my travels, I started to look around for work with which to start the business. I had an appointment with a builder at Woodford and he said that one of his customers was looking for someone to make cabinets for loudspeakers, and he promised to get me an appointment with him. It looked as though things were on the move. Bob, Bert and myself had our meeting; they told me that they had managed to find £150 between them. I was to buy a few small machines, resign from the W. D. C. and start as soon as it was convenient.

The Monday following, I handed in my resignation to my chief who was astonished at my request. I told him I was fed up with working hard for the W. D. C. and getting no results for my efforts. I took my last case of fraud as an example. Nothing had been done. He agreed, said that he couldn't cut the red tape and accepted my resignation. That week I bought the machines and, when they arrived, all three of us went to the workshops and bolted them down in position. We also accepted from Stock's a big workshop that already had some large woodworking machines which we intended to use for trade work. My first order was to make some cabinets for a barbershop. I had to have some help and arranged for a pal of mine to come and work with us. He had a lot of experience and was working for my old boss at the radio cabinet factory. I told him of my intentions and he was only too pleased to turn his job in and start for me. He told me things were just the same there and he was glad to make a change. His name was Dan Packer. I got my resignation confirmed by the head office of the W. D. C. and was wished every success by all the good friends I had made there. I was ready to start on the venture which was to completely alter my life.

CHAPTER TEN

I proudly opened up on my first day and the first thing that happened was a telephone call cancelling the order for the barbershop cabinets. What a start! I had to provide wages for myself and Don Parker, so I needed to get something on the move quick. I went to see a chap who dealt in black market timber and explained my predicament. He helped me out by sending a load of timber for conversion. While Don was getting on with this, I went to see the loudspeaker firm in the East End. I was cordially received and they asked me to make sample cabinets. It was there that I met Ted, who would later play such a large part in my life. He was a partner in a firm who had the sole sales concessions on the firm's loudspeakers. He proved to be one of the most genuine friends it was possible to have.

He promised me he would do his best to get me introductions to several radio firms who might be in need of cabinets. The first few weeks were a struggle but somehow we got by. People started to get to know that we were there and came to us for lots of small jobs. This all helped until I could get something of a more regular nature. I phoned several firms to see if I could be of assistance, and was eventually asked to call in and see the buyer of a big radio corporation in North London. I went along to see him and he asked me if I would care to make 25,000 packing pieces. These were two pieces of wood, $9\frac{1}{2}$in $\times$ 2in $\times$ $\frac{1}{2}$in thick, with four holes drilled in the ends.

They were used to secure plastic radio sets to save any movement in transit. I took the drawing back to the works, made the sample and got the order. This was a step in the right direction. The order was a large one with further prospects of more. The snag was timber. It was very scarce in 1947 and could only be procured on licence. I applied for a licence but was refused as the job wasn't reckoned to be of importance. Bob, Bert and myself agreed we were on the verge of big things. I had to have more help if I was to meet my full commitments. So Bob and Bert decided to give in their notice and come to work with me. I was happy to have them as I felt very lonely. Meantime, all the local spivs were calling in on me either to get something for nothing or sell me a load of stolen timber. Plywood was their speciality. I had a few weeks to make my first delivery of packing pieces, which gave me time to get timber. They wanted the delivery of 2,000 pieces each week. Bob knew his way around and contacted all the dealers who stocked timber. His best success was buying hundreds of bunks that came out of air raid shelters. He got them at a good price and was fully employed knocking them apart. Don was spending most of his time converting them into ½in strips. These were then cut into lengths and made up into cross sections after machining. Mr Stock lent us a small truck which Bob used to do the delivery. The terms of payment were 2½% for cash and Bob had strict instructions *not to come back without the money.*

It wasn't long before the buyer enquired 'as to where he could get a cocktail cabinet cheap.' I knew this was the thin end of the wedge but could do no more than to make him one. This was a racket that went on all the time with these boys. We delivered the cocktail cabinet to his home and I was told that 'I would not regret it.'

We were now getting really busy. One day I was planing some very old black oak on an overhand planer. The timber was very badly twisted and I knew the dangers I was up against, but when struggling in business, one is liable to forget the hazards. I paid dearly for it. I cut the little finger off my left hand. It all happened so fast. Bob rushed over to try and help. We had a first aid kit and he bandaged my hand the best he could. Someone came down the yard and rushed me to hospital. Bob never left me. I was more shocked than anything: to think I had been operating woodworking machines since I was 14 years of age and had never had a serious accident. I was very proud of my hands. Nearly everyone who has worked in sawmills has some part of their fingers missing but I had to wait until I worked for myself to cut my finger off. That was the galling part of it. I had my hand operated on and Bob took me home. The problem was how to tell my wife. Bob broke the news to her very gently and she took it well. It took months for my hand to heal. In the meantime I somehow managed to keep things on the move, and Bob and Bert were doing the share of the work.

We were getting some queer characters down the yard. One day Mr Stock came and introduced a Mr George Strude. He was a hairdresser's appliance mechanic and Mr Stock had let him have one of his sheds in the other yard. He asked us to help him as he'd had a very bad time and was trying to get on his feet. Always willing to help out, we promised we would give any help we could. The first thing he asked us was if he 'could he use our telephone number on his billheads.' We said he could. To look at him, one would think he was worth a million dollars. He was wearing a blue serge suit and a gold wristwatch, looking everything the prosperous businessman should. He promised to see us soon and took his departure.

We were doing alright in our own small way and, at weekends, Bob and I lived it up. We were never big drinkers but we had some enjoyable times. After all, all work makes Jack a dull boy etc, and we had earned it. Things didn't always run smoothly. One Friday morning I was awakened by a loud knocking on the front door. I ran down the stairs half asleep and as I opened the door there stood a great big policeman.

'Mr Jasper?' he said. I told him I was. 'Have you a small factory down the road?' I told him I had, and he said, 'You did have mate, it was burned down during the night and is now a load of ashes.' Too dumbfounded to speak, I asked him in for a cup of tea. As we were drinking the tea, I started to laugh. He looked amazed and asked me what I had to laugh about. After all that had happened to me, what else was there to do but laugh?

What with having my finger off and the continual struggle to survive, I was thankful to be able to laugh. I explained all this to the policeman. He wished me luck. I broke the news to Lilian who, as usual, took it very calmly. I went to the yard and the large workshop was completely gutted. Luckily, the workshop with our completed work inside was intact. At least we had our wages coming. We contacted Mr Stock who came down at once. The big machines were not badly damaged. He sent two men down with a load of scaffolding and some tarpaulin sheets, and in no time at all we were under cover again. It enabled us to keep going. The fire was discovered by an old chap who lived in the next house. He saw it all aglow and opened the door. Immediately the air got to it and it went up in a flash. Fireworks were blamed for the fire but Bob always reckoned it was Don Packer's fault. He was always careless with his cigarettes and Bob told him time and time again about this. There was nothing we could do about it so we made the best of our misfortune. George Strude was now settled in his shed and he gave us his card. He had our number and a Mayfair number. We got many calls for him and some were not of a very friendly nature. He used to arrive about 9 am as though he had just left the Ritz.

Ted gave me a ring one day and asked me to go and see him. When I got there, he said his firm wanted 100 large wooden trays with sections inside for heavy metal parts. These were for the assembly line in the factory. I gave the price of 23/- each and it was accepted. We promised to make delivery by Christmas, which gave us about six weeks to complete the job. We anticipated a good share out for Christmas with our other work and the firm promised to pay us on delivery. Again, timber was our problem. Bob went and got most of it, and the rest we managed to get by hook or crook. Time came when we finished the trays, so I phoned the firm telling them we would send them in next day which was Christmas Eve. Bob delivered and as the last ones were being got off, he asked for the buyer. He gave Bob an envelope. When he got back I opened it eagerly, anticipating our share out. The cheque was there, but it was only for £5. After six months' hard work, we were looking forward to a share-out for Christmas and to have a good time. Instead, nothing.

After Christmas I got in touch with Ted who eventually got the money through for us but I found out that the firm were, like us, struggling and short of cash.

Next, Ted introduced us to a radio rental company. They could not buy cabinets owing to the timber shortage and could not get a licence to make new ones. They had hundreds of old cabinets in stock from before the war, however. I saw the buyer, who gave me a couple of these cabinets and told me to have a go at bringing them up-to-date.

I got back to the workshop to tell Bob and Bert of my problem. These were upright models and terribly out of date, so we decided to knock the bottom off, making it into the side by adding a new piece of plywood. Then, we knocked the front out and added a new one with some light-coloured mouldings. We now had a horizontal cabinet. We stripped off the old polish, cleaned it up and were proud of our effort. We found a polisher who made a good job of it and proudly submitted my sample. I was told I had done a good job and my sample was accepted. I was asked if I could do 50 a week and was astounded at such a large quantity. I said I could and the buyer took me out for a drink. He told me I could have all the work I wanted and 'could I possibly make him a radiogram cabinet?'

'Here we go again,' I thought to myself. What else could I do but offer to make him one? His name was Ted Learner.

I told Bob and Bert of my good fortune. Both agreed we should do the job but it meant that we needed one or two new machines. We also had to have a polishing department. We saw Mr Stock, who suggested we make our business into a Limited Company. He said he would like to come in as a director. Somehow, at the time, we valued his advice. We saw his accountant, a Mr Robert Barton, who made all the legal arrangements.

We got the machines on hire purchase and got cracking on the cabinet job. I think we got 16/- for every cabinet, which was a fair proposition. We needed a cabinetmaker. Many of my old friends, who worked with me at the radio cabinet works, often called in to see me on a Saturday morning. I asked one if he would like a job at 6d an hour over the normal rate. He was a good maker and didn't need asking twice. I explained that conditions were not all that good, yet we hoped to do better as soon as we were established. The cabinets were now starting to come off the line. So our next problem was getting them polished. We tried sending them to a local polisher but he was making a shabby job of them. We were really stuck. How were we going to get over it? We had to have our own polishing department. We took on a couple of sheds in the other yard and set up our own department but it was hard going. We had to load the cabinets onto a builder's handcart and wheel them over to the other yard. What else could we do? Strude had the shed next to us, and was doing radio and electrical repairs. We were now in production and, although we were doing a good job, we were not very happy with the polishing results.

One day, Ted got in touch again and told me to go to a firm in Victoria. They wanted 100 triple holding loudspeaker cabinets for public address on railway stations. They were very large cabinets and had to be finished in maroon paint. I said I could do the job, got the order and explained to Bob and Bert what I had taken on. It was a difficult job but I was more worried about the spraying of the cellulose paint. This is not an easy thing. First, one has to get a licence from the local council. Then the premises have to be fireproofed. A special storage tank had to be installed for storing cellulose too, so we had a real problem on our hands. One day, I was with the polishers when I met Strude. I was explaining our problems to him and he said he knew of a place where he could get a small plug-in electric sprayer for £6 15s 0d.

He said he knew how to do the spraying and that, if I agreed, he would go and get one to spray the cabinets himself. I gave him the money and told Bob and Bert what I had done. They said I would be lucky if I ever saw the money again, let alone the spray. Strude was always short of cash and they reckoned he would come back with some hard-luck story, but to our amazement our wicked thoughts were uncalled for. He came back with the spray. We got the paint and George started spraying. I have never seen anyone in such a state in my life. He had as much paint on his face as he had on the cabinets. The fumes from the spray were going down his throat and he was spitting up maroon paint after every cabinet he sprayed. All the blow from the spray was going over the wall, onto the washing hanging on the lines. It looked like a scene from a Keystone comedy of years ago. If the council had called, we would have all been pinched. All credit must go to George. He made a good job of the cabinets, even if he did swallow more paint than he sprayed onto them. Yet we were now getting what we wanted in finishes, even if we were doing it the hard way.

CHAPTER ELEVEN

We were now getting established, and most of my time was spent going out and getting work. I also had to look after the technical side of the business. The type of work we were undertaking was of a very accurate nature; it was engineering woodwork. With the set-up we had, I look back and marvel how we ever turned out such work. Our greatest problem was finishing and we decided to do something about it. It meant taking a chance, so I went along to see a local cellulose manufacturer and he offered to work for us. The conditions were appalling. It was alright on a dry day, but if the weather was damp we had problems. Considering the snags – the weather, the dust and working without the council finding out – we didn't do too badly.

One morning, I went along to see how Jack the sprayer was getting on. I saw him standing on a box, looking over into someone's garden. He was having a terrific row with a woman whose washing was getting contaminated with fumes from the spray. I had to step in and take over. He was really going to town with this poor woman, telling her to 'get stuffed.' I explained to her that we would soon be moving out and begged her indulgence. She cooled off and I told Jack to do his spraying further up the yard.

At the yard, Strude put a big nameplate on the door: 'G Strude. Electrical, radio and television repairs, etc.' Knowing we were not supposed to have industry of any description in the yard, this looked like an open invitation to any suspicious council employee. I gave him two hours to take it down, which he did very reluctantly. He knew we were not supposed to be there yet he had to do something stupid.

Ted was now introducing me to several radio firms. He would take me on his rounds and give me introductions. He was a good friend to us, was Ted. I was, however, finding the radio trade to be the most cut-throat game in the world. The buyers would argue all day to save a penny and they all expected a 'drop' if they gave you an order. They either wanted cash or something of value. When I had to go to a rental company, it always cost me a couple of pounds for a drink for the buyer.

Word was getting around at my old firm that I was doing alright, and the best men in the trade were coming to me for jobs. They knew I was paying the best wages and, as I wanted them, I gave them jobs. This was getting under the skin of my old boss, whose name I have never mentioned. I have, however, thought of a good name to suit him and by which I can refer to him in the future: Leecher.

One night, Mr Stock was working late in his office when he heard a ring at the door and who should be standing there when he opened it but Leecher. He enquired for me and was told I wasn't there. He wanted to know why I was taking his men away. Stock told him to find out from me. Next day, he phoned me and asked if I would go and see him in three days' time. I told him I would be along. I had nothing to fear. Men were entitled to work where ever they pleased. I was surprised, when I got to Leecher's office, to see half a dozen men sitting round a table. These were members of the big radio cabinetmaker society of Great Britain. I wasn't a member. Leecher completely ignored me and opened the meeting by accusing me of taking his men. I told him and all those present that, 'if a man who satisfies my wants comes to me for a job, I'll take that man, irrespective of where he is working, and if I choose to pay that man better wages, it was entirely my own business.'

'Anyway,' I said, 'fascism ended with the war.' He was livid and strutting about like a peacock. It didn't take the society members long to discuss the matter and give the following decision: 'All members are agreed that Mr Leecher should put his own house in order before complaining about others'. This was a sheer waste of time as far as I was concerned, though to see Leecher's face was worth it.

He looked stupid amongst all the members. Yet Leecher never forgave me for making him look the idiot he was.

We now had about a dozen workers and they were all working hard. We still had plenty of hangers-on who were trying to take us for a ride but they were all left to Bob who usually got the measure of them.

Sometime in June, I went on my usual trip to the polishers to find Strude lying on a camp bed. It was about 8.30 in the morning and he had overslept. I went in and woke him up, and he said he had been there all night. By the look of things, he seemed to have taken up permanent residence. On making enquiries with Jack the sprayer and one or two more, I discovered that he had been sleeping there for over a week. I had a chat with him. He'd had a row with the woman he lived with over money. She'd turfed him out. Having nowhere to go, he thought he would make his residence in the shed. I asked him what he was doing about going to the lavatory and, pointing to a dustbin in the corner of the shed with a piece of plywood for a top, he said 'I am using that.' My chaps were getting worried about the smell, so I told him to get rid of it. I told him the only lavatory I knew was over in the other yard, and it was his business to get it there. I asked Stock about getting Strude evicted and he agreed; Strude was getting to be a pest and would have to go.

About 2 o'clock that afternoon, I had completely dismissed Strude from my mind when suddenly I was confronted by his boy. Poor little fellow was sweating and, as he approached me, he said in a very timid voice, 'I've got it outside.' Looking at the boy and not knowing what to make of him, I said 'got what outside?'

He was terrified. 'It's on the barrow,' he said. Bob and Bert were wondering what this was about. The poor kid was shaking with fear. I looked up the yard and there was Strude's dustbin on a builder's handcart. Strude had let that poor boy push the truck all through the streets with the dustbin full of urine and excrement. I hate to think of what would have happened had it fallen off. I had a word with one of the chaps who volunteered to give the boy a hand. The

sight of Fred emptying the bin down an ordinary lavatory to the sounds of laughter and catcalls had to be seen to be believed. Fred was swearing and cursing at the boy. 'Go and tell your old man he's a dirty rotten bastard!' he said as he started to empty it. I told Strude he would have to get out within a week. Needless to say, within the next week the woman he was living with took him to court on a charge of stealing money and her boy's ration books. The judge slung the book at him and he got six months. Poor Strude, when he came out he called in to see us. I asked him how he got on in the clink and his reply was, 'It's a piece of bleeding cake.' He also reckoned he had got friendly with the governor of Pentonville who was 'sorry to see him go.' That was the last I saw of Strude.

We were now being pressed for room and had to get proper premises before the winter set in. We finally settled on a first-floor factory near Shoreditch. The rent was three times more than we were paying but we had to have it. All our workers came with us and we eventually settled in. Now I had to get more work to cope with our increased overheads. Ted gave me more introductions and I got an order for 2,500 record players for a firm who were agents for a large mail order company. Its two directors were absolutely ruthless, but I got them down to a suitable price and started producing the job. The first 500 went through without a hitch. Suddenly, for no apparent reason, we started to get rejects. I went and saw the directors of the firm and wanted to know why our cabinets were getting rejected. Their explanation was that their inspectors had rejected them and that's all there was to it. I asked if I could see their inspection department and they took me along. The inspectors were unskilled workers who had no knowledge of the trade whatsoever. These people were given a slight idea of what would pass, and, as far as the firm was concerned, their responsibilities were at an end. I told them I had a case if I took it to a court of law; the firm were taking unfair advantage of us. If inspection was needed it should be done by fully-skilled workers. I won my point. I was glad to get the order finished and to get away from those vultures who didn't care a hoot whether you lived or died.

Cancellation of orders was nothing new, there wasn't much one could do about it. Orders were tied up in all sorts of legal mumbo-jumbo and the buyers safeguarded themselves in every way. If they didn't want to pay, their favourite way out was to reject the job. I was learning fast and getting the measure of these sharks, but Bob and Bert were wondering if it was worthwhile to carry on.

We knew a chap who was a designer. His name was Charlie Broadhurst. He designed a record cabinet to match a famous maker's radiogram and submitted his design on paper. They said they liked it and wanted to see a sample cabinet. Charlie asked us to make a cabinet, which we did. It was a beautiful job in exotic veneers. He had great hopes for it but I warned him they had been responsible for more cabinetmakers going broke than I care to mention. Their method was to give an order and expect the impossible where veneers and woodwork were concerned, before rejecting

90% of the work. Charlie would not listen to me. He had visions of orders for thousands of cabinets. When the sample was ready I went with him to submit it. We went to the firm's head office in South East London and met the directors. They studied the cabinet for over an hour and liked it very much. The managing director suggested they send for the chief inspector to get his opinion. 'This is where the fun starts, boy,' I whispered to Charlie. The chief inspector arrived. He was the most surly-looking individual one could wish to meet. He went over the cabinet with microscopic thoroughness. He felt for veneer blisters and held the cabinet up to the light to see if the grain of the veneers had been properly filled in. Meanwhile, Charlie was beginning to understand what I had been trying to tell him all along. The inspector couldn't find any fault. In the end, he got his ruler out and started to measure the grain in the veneers.

'This figuring is out,' he said. I asked him what he meant. 'The grain of the veneer of the right half of the top is wider than the grain of the left half,' he replied. I had never heard such a statement in my life. This was utter nonsense from a man who had a position as chief inspector and whose stupid decisions could and did send manufacturers bankrupt.

I lost my temper. 'I have no control whatever over the growth of the bloody trees,' I said. Turning to Charlie and speaking loudly so all could hear, I said, 'Satisfied mate? What did I tell you? Give me a hand to get this in the car.' We both lifted the cabinet out of the place without saying another word. Near London Bridge, Charlie realised that what I had been telling him for weeks had come true. He pulled up, took me to the nearest pub and said, 'Stan, have the best lunch in the house, you've saved me a fortune.'

When I got back, and told Bob and Bert of our experience, they realised we were in the wrong trade. Bob had been wanting to get out for some time. He saw an advertisement in the *Evening News* for someone who was looking to buy a woodwork business. He replied to it. We all decided to get out if the offer was good enough.

They drove a hard bargain and there wasn't much left to share out after we had paid our debts, but we all parted the best of friends and much wiser from our experience. Bob was going to have six months' rest and Bert was going in with a friend, pattern-making. As for myself, I decided to carry on where we had started. I got the rental company to let me have some more cabinets for re-polishing and began all over again.

CHAPTER TWELVE

I was now entirely on my own. During the ensuing week, I took over the two polishing sheds. I made one into a workshop and the other into a polishing shop. I put a down payment on a compressor, fixed up benches and racks, and was all ready to start again.

My eldest son was now demobbed from the forces and I took him in with me. I also managed to get a woman polisher who had previously worked for us. Now I was getting cabinets from the rental company for repair and re-polishing. Ted Learner, the buyer, came to see me and asked me if he could look after my books. He said he knew all about getting books ready for the accountants. I saw what he was up to but was reliant on him for work and agreed to let him do the books for a fee of £2 a week. It wasn't long before my old business associates found out where I was. Ted came to see me and advised me to try and pick up the threads where I left off, but this wasn't easy as I had no proper premises. I was only set up for repairs.

We had to keep the gates of the yard locked in case anyone from the council happened to be passing. I had a bell fitted and it was only after the special code we devised was rung that we would open the gates. If the bell was rung by anyone that didn't know the code, it gave us a chance to put the spray under cover. As time went on, I wasn't doing too badly and several radio firms were asking me to repair damaged cabinets. I was getting more work than I could handle but the conditions we were working under were terrible.

After a few months the council got to know that we were using a spray, so I had to find premises that were scheduled for our type of industry.

One day, I was talking to a chap who had a fish and chip shop near where I was living, telling him of my predicament in trying to find a place to work. 'Why don't you try the factory next door?' he said. He told me that it had been bought as an investment and the owners were letting it out in three sections. I saw the owners and they offered me the first floor at £8 per week. Although it had already been used for spraying by the previous owners, the rent was more than I was prepared to pay. I had to make my mind up there and then, otherwise someone else would come and take it. I had no Bob with me to discuss this with and had to decide alone, so I agreed to take the place. It had to be fitted out with suction fans to clear the spray fumes, flameproof lighting and storage space built for storing cellulose. My first plan was to contact the council and confirm that it had been used for my trade by the previous owners.

I went to the Town and Country Planning department of the town hall, and was directed to an official who dealt with cases like mine. He told me it would take months for the matter to be brought up in front of the council and, even then, he could not guarantee that it would be passed. He took me to one side, telling me he would stay late that night and that I should bring the file concerning the premises I wanted. If the work I wanted done was scheduled, he would get it passed immediately. I told him the owners had already stated that the factory was scheduled for my class of industry, which was why I was there to get confirmation. I gave him a fiver and, within three days, I got a letter to the effect that the premises were scheduled for spraying.

It was a pleasure to work in our new factory. Everything was nice and clean, and we were working without being chased by the council. My second son was now out of the forces and he started work with us. He was a good woodworker and an asset to us. Ted was introducing me to several firms for repair work and we were doing very well. I now had six of us at work and the place was getting stacked with cabinets of all sorts. Work was coming in from all over the place.

Other firms were now asking me to make cabinets for them too. I had no way of doing this yet I hated the idea of turning work away.

I agreed to take on small orders for the smaller cabinets and farmed them out to various small firms to make. Now I had a full time job going round to the subcontractors, keeping them up to scratch. This was not easy, as it was very hard to convey the very fine standards they had to work to.

The radio manufacturers were finding it very difficult to get cabinetmakers to work for them after the filthy tricks they played on the industry. They were now trying to buy up established cabinet firms and make their own cabinets to ease the position. One of the largest radio firms in the country bought the controlling interest in many cabinet works. Once any firm signed a contract with them, they were well and truly trapped. Without the slightest excuse, they would reject cabinets by the hundreds, especially if they were short of cash. Consequently, if the firm wasn't big enough, they went to the wall. I got trapped myself.

One day, I was sent two cabinets that had been badly damaged from a well-known firm at Hayes. We repaired and re-polished them to such a standard that no one could tell the difference when they were compared with new cabinets. I hired a car and took them to Middlesex, asking for the gent concerned, and was taken up to his office. They really treated me like a human being. I wasn't used to this kind of treatment. The gentleman I saw was a Mr Goodwright. He was a fine chap. He sent down for the cabinets and went over them with two of his inspectors.

'Here we go, this is it!' I thought to myself. I was wrong. They were delighted and said that, if I kept up that standard of work, I could have a weekly supply of cabinets. There was no haggling over price. They would deliver and inspect at my factory. 'I must be dreaming,' I thought, nearly collapsing. Never had I been treated like this in my life, it was the beginning of an understanding that was to last for a long time.

We had our differences, like all firms. They were a 100% trade union firm. Word got around that I was taking some of their work and the shop stewards wanted to know what wages I was paying my workers. I was asked to go and explain my point of view at a meeting of the shop stewards. I showed my wages book, and they saw that I was paying over the trade union rate. Regarding conditions, I invited them over to see my place and the set-up. This seemed to satisfy them and the matter was dropped.

Every trip I took to Middlesex was a royal occasion. I got to know many people over there and we nearly always went out to the local pub for lunch. I got an introduction to the secretary of the firm, a Mr Hutton. As soon as we were introduced, we somehow took to each other. He was a self-educated man, born and bred in the East End of London. We soon got round to discussing our childhood, our upbringing and the localities we had lived in. We became firm friends.

My wife and I were getting invitations to the homes of some of these people but it was very awkward for us to return these invitations as we were still living in a council house. I decided that something had to be done about this and in 1950 had enough money to put down a deposit on my first house. The house we bought wasn't too far away from the factory and we were now in a position to reciprocate these invitations.

I bought a new car and had a chap to drive me around, although I'd had a driving license for many years. My business appointments somehow always finished up with a few drinks and I never felt justified to drive whilst under the influence of drink. At last, life was being good to me. I thought I was set up for the future. I had found many friends and couldn't go wrong, or so I thought. I saw Ted Learner from the rental company every week but he had become an alcoholic.

I always had to spend a minimum of two hours with him in the pub. It cost me a lot of money and wasted time, which was getting very important to me. Sometimes he would ask for a bottle of gin to take home. 'You can afford it,' he would say. He knew because he kept my books. This was now more or less blackmail. We got to know his wife, and were very sorry for her due to his excessive drinking. She had a lot to put up with. I once visited them and got to his home before he arrived from his office. He was so drunk that he fell flat on his face as he attempted to get out of his car. He had several accidents but said none of them were his fault, yet I couldn't break it off with him as he was still getting me a lot of work. It was such a pity as he was the nicest chap one could ever wish to meet, when he was sober.

I was still seeing my old friend Bob. We had many good outings together, but my life was getting hectic. One day, I decided I ought to get life insurance. I wanted my family to be well-covered should anything happen to me. I made an application and was sent a letter telling me to attend a medical examination. I went along to the doctor and, after being examined, I was told I would be informed of the result by letter. A few days later, I got a letter from the insurance company telling me that under no circumstances could they insure me. This really shook me. I phoned the doctor who had examined me, asking him why he had turned me down.

He told me to see my own doctor, so I asked him if he would see me as a private patient, to which he agreed and gave me an appointment. He told me that I had an enlarged heart and severe hypertension. He advised me to take life very easy. He offered to look after me, and give me all the advice and attention he could.

From that day in 1952 until the present day, he has kept his word. By his attention and sincerity, he has helped keep me alive. He also proved to be one of the sincerest friends I have ever had. It wasn't easy to break the news to my family.

After discussion, it was agreed I that I should take things easier. There wasn't much else I could do but take it easy, as I was under very heavy sedation to get the blood pressure down. My boys took over for a time but it was a tough game for them as they didn't have the experience to deal with the sharks in the trade. We had many ups and downs but, taking things by and large, we were steadily progressing. I heard of some very nice houses that were being built near the forest and the district appealed to me. My wife and I went along and we chose the first one to be ready, paid the deposit on the spot and awaited the completion.

When it was finished, it looked marvellous. We bought everything new and moved in. We were highly delighted with our new home and our circle of friends was expanding. My wife warned me about many of them but I never look for faults in people. To me, everyone is okay until I find them otherwise.

CHAPTER THIRTEEN

I was being pressed by many firms to make cabinets. Restrictions had been lifted by the Conservative government on deposits and a boom ensued. I had two subcontractors working for me as well as two places of my own.

I could not keep going to the subcontractors and keeping them up to scratch. This was a highly skilled job and inspection was essential. My health would not stand up to this, so I decided to look around one or two factory estates that were being developed. I came across an industrial estate in Essex and decided to build a factory there. I had plans drawn up and passed by the local council for a modern woodworking factory covering half an acre. I installed the latest machinery and facilities for my workers that were second to none in the trade.

A housing estate was going up in the district and most of my workers agreed to move into new houses as they became available. Within six months, the factory was finished and we moved in. I had a full order book and many more workers were needed. It didn't take long for word to get around and, before I knew it, I had over 70 men, women and lads working for me. The shops were open and I welcomed members of the trade unions. I now had two typists, a manager and my old accountant working full-time.

I was very proud of my achievements and it seemed that my dreams were coming true. Timber went in one end of the factory and the finished products came out the other. I was getting noted in the trade for a high standard of workmanship. My wife and family were against what I was doing, due to the declining state of my health, but I felt I had to carry on.

In 1955, the government started the first of a series of 'Stop Go' budgets. This caused higher deposits on radio and television sets, and many of my orders were cancelled. We survived three of these 'Stop Go' periods but I hated to sack my workers. I had an offer from a well known television company to take my place over. They offered me £8,000, payment of all debts owed by the company, a seat on their board of directors, a salary of £1,500 per annum to be available when I was required for advice etc, a car and hotel expenses, and my wife looked after in the event of anything happening to me.

My wife and family told me to take it, owing to my health, but I had faith in what I was doing. All my capital was tied up with the banks as a guarantee for overdrafts. I also wanted to try and do the right thing by those who were loyal and had stuck by me. My experience of takeovers always meant bringing in new blood, and the old and trusted workers being slung out on their necks.

I decided to hang on and try to weather the storm. All around me on the estate many factories, especially woodworkers, were closing their doors. In December 1955, I was called in by a well known firm of television manufacturers regarding further work. I had done thousands of cabinets for this firm and was well received by the directors whenever I went there. They always laid out the red carpet for me and treated me as part and parcel of the firm.

We had our usual Christmas party, and I was given an order for 10,000 Console Television Cabinets. This represented a turnover of £120,000. Not a bad way to start the New Year, considering there was a slump on. Before leaving, I was called into the managing director's office and shown a cabinet that came from the continent. This firm also had their own cabinet workers but couldn't turn out a half of the cabinets they needed. They asked what I thought of it. I was told they were importing 500 per week and that their own cabinet works told them that it could not be produced anywhere in this country as it was made on special machinery only available abroad. The managing director told me that if I could produce that cabinet, I was made for life. It was a challenge I accepted. I took one back to my works and told him I would do my best.

After the Christmas holiday I called the works manager, the foreman of the mill, the cabinetmakers and the polishers into my office. We discussed the matter and it was agreed we would have a go at producing it. It took us six weeks to make special jigs and adapt some machines but we made it. I had special mouldings flown over from Belgium and our finished cabinet was definitely as good, if not better, than the continental one. We were very pleased with our efforts. I sent the cabinets to the firm concerned, who were amazed that we had achieved what their own works could not produce.

I was told that the cabinets were to be shown to a meeting of the full board of directors and to await results. Two weeks later, I got the result. I received a letter cancelling all outstanding orders for the firm and no word whatsoever about the new cabinets we had submitted. This was the greatest shock of my life. On enquiring the reason, I was told it was due to a trade recession. They told me they would pay for all work I had finished and partly finished, and when I had the list complete, they asked if I would I personally submit my claim for payment. This was the bitterest blow I ever suffered in my life. I had no other orders and there was only one thing left for me to do: shut the factory down. The day I closed and gave my workers notice was a day that remains in my memory. I was heartbroken. All I had worked for was gone. Workers who were like brothers to me were put off.

I was lucky to survive for as long as I did. To make matters worse, I could not get a full explanation as to why the firm had cancelled all the orders. I intended to find out; I had the final figures for the finished works and works-in-progress, and went along to see them. It was an atmosphere I shall never forget.

CHAPTER FOURTEEN

On arrival at the works, I was told no one was available. The firm's accountant would see me, however. I was not even shown into his office. Instead, a table and chairs were set out in a space outside the office, and I discussed the final accounts with him there. While we were discussing the accounts, I could see various people dodging below glass partitions in order to avoid me. I never felt so humiliated in my life. Men who I had wined and dined with were now afraid to show their faces. I wanted the floor to open up and swallow me. I settled my accounts and was promised prompt payment.

Bankruptcy was now staring me in the face. I was taken ill with heart trouble and was in hospital for quite some time. The firm went into liquidation during my hospital stay. I went to the law courts when I was discharged, to try and stop it, but the judge would not listen to me.

I addressed a meeting of creditors and the matter was placed in the hands of an accountant. The sharks started to surface. My new factory was sold with all the machinery to two sharks for £4,500 in one day and bought by a radio manufacturer the next day for £9,000. Everything went for a song. A liquidator was appointed. The bank took all my security as well as my wife's. I sold my house to meet my commitments. I had to appeal to the housing committee of the local council for help. In the past, I had helped many families from the district get rehoused. They considered my application sympathetically and gave us a flat.

I had several friends who were trying to find out the truth as to why my orders were cancelled from the radio and television corporation responsible for my downfall. I got the truth at last from a thoroughly reliable source.

The two cabinets I had made were sent to the head office, and a high-level directors' meeting was called. On the board of directors was an old enemy of mine who was responsible for all woodwork. He was jealous of my success. He was the individual who had previously told the board that the cabinet could not be produced in this country. The meeting started with four cabinets. Each director was asked to say 'which were the foreign cabinets, and which were the English ones.' Upon examination, not one of them could tell the difference. The chairman then turned to the jealous director, saying, 'You, with all the resources of the company, told us the cabinet cannot be produced in this country. Yet a small firm has produced it. What have you to say?' He was so indignant and powerful that he gave instructions for the cancellation of any orders I had from the firm.

I was forced to give up in 1962 owing to the state of my health. My son is now working at a large London furniture works, getting a good and regular wage. As for myself, I am living on a National Health Disablement Pension plus a grant for my rent from the National Security Board. In the past six years, I have been in hospital more times than I care to remember with heart attacks, the removal of an artery, a haemorrhage of the lungs and severe hypertension. Yet I still think life is good and I have many of my old friends who regularly call in from Hoxton, Shoreditch, and Hackney.

I look back on my past, now I have all the time in the world to think. I am very fortunate with what I have. I have a wonderful wife and three sons. They call in every day to see us. They are very good to us. I have what money cannot buy: love and understanding.

CONCLUSION

I look back to when I was a boy, when I had just left school and I started working in a sawmill in London's East End.

It was a filthy, dust-ridden hole full of antiquated and dangerous machinery. I worked with a square-block one-hand planer, the most dangerous machine that man could devise. In its place now is the motorised circular-block high-speed machine. The old grease-bearing planing machine left ripples in the planks, piling up wood chips from floor to ceiling. In its place today sits a high speed motorised machine with its own extraction plant. Not a chip to be seen anywhere.

The old ground off saw-bench required brute strength to push the planks through the saw. The boy at the back was given a thick wedge and hammer and, when the plank passed the back of the saw, he hammered in the wedge to save the saw from bending. Yet today, we see saws cut up trees into planks as easily as slicing up a loaf of bread. One could go on and on.

The accident rate was terrible then. Unguarded cutters took off many a finger and the filth and dust caused bronchitis and tuberculosis. How different today. It was a long and hard fight for these improvements, but get them we did.

I have often been asked two important questions.

Question 1: If I were a young man in this day and age, 'Would I still be a militant trade unionist?'

The answer is 'YES', and more so today than ever before. It took years of hard work and negotiation to achieve the conditions in existence today, but there is still plenty of room for improvement.

Question 2: "Would I start in business again if I were a young man?"

I find this a very difficult question. If I did make up my mind to start in business, I would have to be ruthless, cunning and crafty. I would also have to study psychology. I would find out how to obtain the lowest prices from my suppliers, while letting them think I am a fine chap and giving them all the help I could muster. But I would prefer to be a normal human being with the love of my family and friends, especially those from my childhood days in Hoxton, in the East End of London.

AFTERWORD

AFTERWORD

The Gentle Author visited A. S. Jasper's only surviving son Terry Jasper in Loughton to ask about his father's life and the background to his writing.

THE GENTLE AUTHOR: What do your father's initials stand for?

TERRY JASPER: A for Albert and S for Stanley, but he was always know as Stan, never Albert.

THE GENTLE AUTHOR: Did he speak to you about his early life in Hoxton?

TERRY JASPER: He used to talk about his childhood quite a lot, he never forgot it. My dad had a very good memory and he more or less remembered everything that happened to him. So my uncle Bob said, 'Why don't you write it all down?' and he did. But then he tried to get it published without success. I only became aware of the manuscript of *A Hoxton Childhood* when he told me that he had not had any response to his attempts to have it published. At the time, I was working at W. W. Sprague, a printing firm in City Road. They were long-established and had printed the first Penny Black stamp. I mentioned my dad's book to a young fellow I worked with there, he knew someone who worked for the publishers Barrie & Rockliff, and they really liked it and that was how it got published. When the book came out in 1969, he wanted to go back to Hoxton to see what was still left but his health was not good enough.

THE GENTLE AUTHOR: Did he ever take you to Hoxton?

TERRY JASPER: No, he never did. When I was growing up, we were

187

living in Walthamstow and he was working hard. Once every two or three weeks, we used to go and see his older sister Mary in Stoke Newington and he gave her some money to get by. Her husband was always there, he was a small guy who wore a cap all the time and a shirt with no collar. Florrie, his middle sister, we saw quite a bit of her too. She lived in Edmonton and we used to go over there every few weeks and, whenever he was there, he would always go in and see how his mum was and help her out with some money.

THE GENTLE AUTHOR: Do you remember your grandmother?

TERRY JASPER: I was ten when she died and I only saw her three or four times, when we went over to Flo's for parties. Yet even then she would keep to herself in her own house next door. When dad would go and visit her, I went with him. I always remember once she asked him to take a look for something and he went outside leaving us alone. She just said to me, 'He's my best boy.' She obviously thought a lot of him and he described her as 'The most wonderful woman in the world.'

My grandmother, Johanna Haykins, was born in Amsterdam and both her parents were professional musicians but her father died quite young, and in the 1870s her mother came to England with the three children. Why they decided to come to London, I do not know.

THE GENTLE AUTHOR: Did you father speak about your grandfather?

TERRY JASPER: Dad had a funny way of putting it, he said his mother told him his father was 'more sinned against than sinning.' She was incredibly loyal and I suppose she meant he had more bad things done to him than he did to others, yet it was no excuse for him to carry on the way he did. He was an alcoholic and the poverty of the family was entirely his doing. It was suggested that the reason for this could have been due to the suffering he may have incurred as a child but I do not believe this.

His father came from a long line of agricultural workers who lived in the village of Great Easton, North Essex and his parents were forced to move to London in the 1850s due to the mechanisation of farming which made hundreds of farm workers redundant. Looking at the census records from the time he was born, it appeared he had a relatively normal family life. Even if this was not quite the case, you would think that any hardship he might have endured would then make him determined that this was not going to happen to his own family.

Between 1910 and 1919, the family had to move house eight times, always due to the fact that they were unable to pay the rent. Prior to my father's birth in 1905, goodness knows how many more times they moved for the same reason.

I do not know where he and my grandmother met, but I know she loved dancing and they used to go dancing together. Her mother was strict and she had to be home by a certain time. One evening, she got home late and her mother would not let her in, so they went to his place and she finished up in the family way.

To be honest, I think she just picked the wrong one.

THE GENTLE AUTHOR: Do you think your grandmother felt she had any choice but to stay with your grandfather?

TERRY JASPER: For the sake of the family, I do not think she thought she had any choice other to stay with him. She was a machinist and had to make clothes just to get by, to try and buy some food because he would not give her anything. Trouble was, he was very crafty in-as-much he knew she was making some money sewing clothes – so whatever he was giving her, he would stop giving it to her. It is all very sad really and I do not suppose they were the only family like that.

THE GENTLE AUTHOR: What do you think your father took from his childhood?

TERRY JASPER: I think it taught him the difference between right and wrong, but that came from his mother not his father of course. My dad was somebody who, even when he had a big business, could always talk to people – whether they were the general manager or the guy who cleaned the toilets. I remember in the late sixties, when my mum and dad lived in a small ground floor flat, he looked out of the window into the garden one morning and saw a tramp lying on the grass. My dad took him a sandwich and a cup of tea, and told him that he would not be able to stay there. I think most people in that situation would have just phoned the police and left it at that.

My dad could be quite rash with money sometimes. One occasion was when he went out to buy a new car and came home in a new Hillman Minx convertible with the roof down. He called my mum out to take a look but, on seeing it, she told him that there was no way that she was going to go out in it and, with that, he returned the car to the garage and bought something else. He was always one who, when he had the money, if some new gadget came on the market he would get it.

Anything I wanted, he would buy me if he could afford it. When I was about fourteen, I played a lot of tennis and I saw this tennis racquet I wanted in the window of the sports shop. It was seven guineas which was a lot of money then. I said, 'I'd really like that,' and he said to my mum, 'Seven guineas, that's a hell of a lot of money,' but he bought it for me.

Sometime we used to go out for the day on Sundays. One Sunday we went to the coast, I think it was Clacton. There were a large number of American soldiers standing around, awaiting further orders. All the white boys were in one group and the blacks in another, on the other side of the road. People talking to the white soldiers. However, the black boys were just standing there with nobody around them, so my dad made a point of going over and engaging them in conversation.

THE GENTLE AUTHOR: It is a bitter irony that your father's enlightened sense of how he wanted to live his life was undercut by the health problems he acquired as a boy.

TERRY JASPER: Yes, he had bronchitis right from when he was a lad of fourteen, working in sawmills where there was dust everywhere which got onto his chest. He was told a number of times he should get another job, something outdoors, but he said there were no jobs before the war. He was the only money earner, so he could not just take any job because he had to provide, first for his mother's family and then for his own. He did not receive his first paid holiday until 1939 and, even then, it was only half a week's wages.

When I was about eight years old, he had just had a bout of bronchitis and was given a stern warning from his doctor to pack up what he was doing otherwise it would kill him. My mother, who very rarely said anything, said 'You've got to do what he tells you.' My father was sitting in the armchair and he broke down, just suddenly burst into tears. My mother comforted him. I had never seen a grown up cry before, let alone my dad. I just did not think grown ups cried. Fortunately, he managed to find a different job after that, with the War Damage Commission.

In the mid-fifties, he was advised by his doctor to go away for a holiday to a warmer climate but he knew that my mum would not go. So, in the end, I went with him to San Sebastian. It was March and, when we arrived, there was snow on the ground yet luckily the weather turned out fine and we managed to have quite a nice time.

I never knew him to be down about it. I saw him in and out of hospital numerous times and, once or twice, he broke down but he never moaned.

THE GENTLE AUTHOR: What do you remember of the war?

TERRY JASPER: I was born on December 1st 1936 in Walthamstow and my earliest recollections are of air raids. Everyone in our road had a shelter and this is where we had to spend our nights during the bombing. They were terrible places, condensation ran down the walls and the air smelled of damp. Thousands of children were evacuated out of London including my two older brothers, Stan and Ron. My father gave Stan a stamped addressed envelope to take with him and told him, if for any reason they were not happy, to post it back to him. They finished up in Wales staying with an old couple who had no interest in either of them. They were both very unhappy, so Stan posted off the letter back to dad who stopped everything he was doing, caught the train to where they were staying and brought them back home to London.

THE GENTLE AUTHOR: How did the changes in your father's fortunes affect your childhood?

TERRY JASPER: We lived in a number of council houses but, once he got this job on the War Damage Commission, we always had enough money for meals and things that we wanted. We were never really hard up. Also, my older brother was at home so there was enough money coming in for what we needed.

Eventually, my dad started his own business and, after a while, money became more plentiful. He would always buy us things that we wanted and he was very supportive of me playing football or cricket at school. He would accompany me on away matches, sometimes to travelling to the other side of London.

After he started his own business and got these orders coming in, then he bought his first house in Walthamstow. My two brothers worked for him as well. My older brother Stan used to do all the spraying and he had about eight or nine people working for him then. It was going very well indeed.

THE GENTLE AUTHOR: How did you come to work for your father?

TERRY JASPER: I left school at sixteen and a half but I knew I was due for my call up for National Service in eighteen months time so I did not want to take an apprenticeship because then I would go in the forces at twenty-two or twenty-three which I did not want to do. I decided to work at my dad's place until I was due to be called up. It was quite hard work and the conditions were pretty bad. I had to take the polish off these radio cabinets with paint stripper which made me very light-headed, as if I had had quite a few drinks. My eldest brother Stan used to work a sanding machine and the cabinets would go through various stages of polishing until they came out the other end.

THE GENTLE AUTHOR: Why did it all come to grief?

TERRY JASPER: In the late fifties, a credit squeeze meant the cancellation of large orders and he had over seventy people working for him at the time which worried him considerably. He was offered an excellent financial package for himself by another company which he should have taken. Everybody told him to accept it, but he tried to carry on and save the jobs of his workers. In the end, the situation became hopeless and he was declared bankrupt.

I think he realised that, if he had sold his company, chances were the new owners would have closed it and he wanted to make sure his employees kept their jobs. Obviously, it is all very well thinking about other people but he did not think of himself. He should have taken the offer. The biggest mistake he made was to put my mother on the board of directors. If she had have stayed out of it then, when he went bankrupt, he could have signed the house over to her but instead he finished with more or less absolutely nothing. He lived in a one-bedroom council flat for the rest of his life.

THE GENTLE AUTHOR: Your father's tenacity and generosity of spirit in the face of such relentless disappointment verge on the heroic.

TERRY JASPER: Some of those he worked with before the war, when money was tight, were dishonest and he encountered these people throughout his working life. I think the War Damage Commission job suited him down to the ground but, even there, the people in charge were on the fiddle, so he felt he had not made any progress. If he only had the right people above him then I think he could have made something of that job.

THE GENTLE AUTHOR: Was your father a political man?

TERRY JASPER: We always had two papers in the forties, the *Daily Worker* and the *News Chronicle*. In those years immediately following the war, nobody was aware of Stalin's atrocities in the Soviet Union. My Uncle Bob and him would have a few drinks at home and the toast was always, 'Good old Joe!' – Joe Stalin. To them, he was the one who more or less saved us.

THE GENTLE AUTHOR: What do you think he would have thought of the changes in Hoxton after the war, the slum clearances and the new council estates?

TERRY JASPER: I think he would have been all for it. He knew what some of those old places were like, outside toilets and no bathrooms. It was a different world. After the war, they built prefab houses and people thought they were fantastic because they had a fridge and every modern convenience. It was terrific compared to what they had been used to. I am sure he would have welcomed that.

THE GENTLE AUTHOR: When did your father start writing?

TERRY JASPER: He never started until the early sixties and it was a godsend for him because he could not do any other work.

THE GENTLE AUTHOR: When you first read *A Hoxton Childhood* what were your feelings?

TERRY JASPER: Some of the things in the book he had told me but there were also a lot he had not. It made me feel fortunate that I had the life that I have and did not have to go through what he did. It was such a shame really because his father earned money and they could have had a fairly normal life if he had been a decent kind of fellow. I suppose these days his mum would have said 'on your way' or she would have left him, but they did not do that then.

I mean she must have known what he was like right from the start when he gave her the wedding ring made of brass.

THE GENTLE AUTHOR: Was your father's writing a form of vindication for him?

TERRY JASPER: Yes, my dad passed away in 1970 when he was sixty-five, just a year after the publication of *A Hoxton Childhood* but he saw it was a success.

After he died, my mum lived on in the flat yet people did not come round so often. He was the type to keep the family together more or less. Even when they were living in the one-bedroom flat, a lot of relatives would come to see mum and dad, on my mum's side as well. While he was there, he was the life and soul of the party. I think it was in his make up that people took to him.

He always enjoyed throwing a party, especially if he was in the company of my mother's family. It was not easy obtaining beer and spirits during the war but somehow he managed to find a supply, and he had a nice voice and did not need much persuading to get up and sing a song or two. If he could have a joke about something he would do, and his sisters too – taking the mickey out of the old man and all that. They would always find a laugh and a joke, even in a tragic situation.

I suppose a party was one way of forgetting the ravages of war. I saw him on numerous occasions in a very merry mood yet that was as far as it went. Throughout his life he never turned to violence like his father.

After my dad died, his papers were passed on to my older brothers who both lived locally. It was not until after my last brother died five years ago that these papers – including the manuscript of *The Years After* – were passed to me.

There are a million things I would like to have asked my dad when he was alive but I did not.

He earned some royalties for *A Hoxton Childhood*. By then, he did not have much money yet he always insisted on sharing out the earnings between me and my two brothers. The success of his book gave him a new lease of life, although unfortunately his health was not up to it.

He always said he would settle for the way life turned out.

Stanley Jasper and his son Terry
in Rayleigh, Essex 1956

ACKNOWLEDGEMENTS

This edition, comprising a reprint of *A Hoxton Childhood* with James Boswell's illustrations from the original 1969 edition accompanied by the first publication of the sequel *The Years After* illustrated by Joe McLaren, has been published with the support of Terry Jasper, the author's son. Terry Jasper wishes to thank Richard Penny and Lynda Finn for their contributions.

Spitalfields Life Books is grateful to Sal Shuel for access to James Boswell's artwork, permitting new reproductions of her father's illustrations. Also thanks are due to Walter Donohue for editorial assistance, and to Sydney Diack and So-Shan Au for copy-editing and proofreading.

ALSO PUBLISHED BY SPITALFIELDS LIFE BOOKS

Travellers' Children in London Fields
Colin O'Brien

The Gentle Author's London Album

Brick Lane
Phil Maxwell

Underground
Bob Mazzer

Spitalfields Nippers
Horace Warner

London Life
Colin O'Brien

Baddeley Brothers

The Gentle Author's Cries of London

East End
John Claridge

The Boss of Bethnal Green: Joseph Merceron,
The Godfather of Regency London
Julian Woodford